The
CHESTNUT
Cook Book

RECIPES, FOLKLORE AND PRACTICAL INFORMATION

Written and Illustrated
by
Annie Bhagwandin

HATS
OFF™

Third edition (2003) published by Hats Off Books™
610 East Delano Street, Suite 104, Tucson, Arizona 85705, U.S.A.
www.hatsoffbooks.com

Publisher's Cataloging-in-Publication
(Provided by Quality Books, Inc.)

Bhagwandin, Annie.
    The chestnut cook book : recipes, folklore and practical information / written and illustrated by Annie Bhagwandin. -- 3rd ed.
    p. cm.
    LCCN 2002096377
    ISBN 1-58736-167-1

    1. Cookery (Chestnuts)   2. Chestnut.   I. Title.

TX814.2.C48B45 2004   641.6'453
                                 QBI03-200262

The "Chestnut of a Hundred Horsemen" once sheltered Jeanne of Aragon and her entourage from a summer storm and is the largest, if not oldest, living chestnut tree. Sicily

A s I stand in the midst of a small grove of 150 year old chestnut trees my feelings overwhelm me. The strong smell of autumn pervades as I relish each moment in this protective canopy. The strength and abundance of these trees help me feel whole, human and very much a part of this earth, as I silently thank the people who planted them so many years ago.

I hope this cookbook inspires not only your appetite, but also your desire to plant more of these majestic trees.

FOREWORD

The first chestnut tree I ever saw was a seedling grown from a seed I planted myself when I was about 15 years old. I had received a dozen or so nuts to plant from my neighbor, John Todd, of the New Alchemy Institute in Woods Hole, Massachusetts. John told me they were American chestnuts. He got them from Dick Jaynes at the Connecticut Agricultural Experiment Station in New Haven. I planted the seeds in flowerpots in a little lean-to greenhouse and a year later John and I moved them to a nursery bed that we dug in his back yard. From the nursery bed, most of the trees were moved to the New Alchemy farm in Hatchville, but I set out one of them in my front yard in Sippewissett, where it is still growing.

When my first chestnut tree was about a year old, I read Tree Crops: A Permanent Agriculture, by J. Russell Smith. The book made a lot of sense to me. At the time, the late 1970s, I was concerned about the end of oil, overpopulation, and world hunger. Tree Crops offered practical examples of real solutions to many of the problems of agriculture: soil erosion, increased fertilizer costs, harmful pesticides, and the loss of biological diversity. On sloping or mountainous land, nut-bearing trees and other woody crop species may be the only sustainable solution to producing food. Of all the kinds of tree crops discussed by J. Russell Smith, the chestnuts were by far the most fascinating to me. I was especially moved by Smith's description of the thousands-of-years-old chestnut groves in Italy and on the island of Corsica, a veritable chestnut civilization. It may be an exaggeration to claim that the European chestnut tree represents one of the columns upon which Western civilization was built—but it would only be a slight exaggeration—and certainly the chestnut ranks right up there with the grapevine and the olive tree as a Mediterranean staple. Chinese and Japanese chestnut trees played similar, and no less important, roles in the East Asian civilizations of China, Korea, and Japan.

It was during the seven years I lived in northern Italy that I had my most significant chestnut experiences. Learning about chestnuts, listening to the Italians talk about their chestnuts, listening to their shared memories of the chestnut forests, of chestnut trees, of recipes, of the tannin extraction, of the famine during the wars and how at the end of the war the chestnut tree was all they had, I came to appreciate the cultural values, the historic values, the personal values, the landscape values, and the intrinsic values that the tree represents to peoples of Italy, and I came to appreciate the enormity of the tragedy that would befall the earth if this heritage were lost. And I decided I wanted to learn more about chestnut trees.

The twentieth century was hard on the chestnut, particularly in Europe and North America. A conspiracy of circumstances, catastrophic diseases, two world wars, cultural revolutions, changing diets, and the almost insane economics of the global village have contributed to the near total loss of the American chestnut, significant erosion of European and Asian chestnut genetic resources, and the near extinction of the chestnut civilization worldwide. But chestnut trees are once again being planted, all over the world, in the places that chestnuts have been grown traditionally, and in the places where chestnut growing has been only recently introduced. Advances in plant breeding and molecular biology promise us blight-resistant chestnut trees. New (and newly rediscovered) knowledge about the ecological benefits of tree crops makes more sense now than ever before. Exciting new marketing opportunities are opening up to chestnut growers around the globe that allow farmers and consumers alike to benefit from locally grown and locally processed chestnuts.

Chestnuts can be, and should be, a part of a healthy diet and a healthy agriculture. The Chestnut Cook Book by Annie Bhagwandin is a significant contribution to chestnut culture in the English-speaking world. Annie has drawn from a broad diversity of cultural and ethnic traditions from all of the world's chestnut civilizations, collecting and testing recipes, for her cookbook. The result is a work that will encourage wider use of the chestnut for generations to come.

J. Hill Craddock

Table of Contents

INTRODUCTION

Due to the resurging interest in chestnuts as a viable orchard crop not only in the United States, but around the globe, it seems appropriate to dedicate a cookbook to the fruit of such a noble tree. My personal experiences with chestnuts began while I was a college student in Bloomington, Indiana. Every Fall as the Harvest moon approached, my friends and I would scout out our favorite fruit and nut trees within bicycle distance of town in anticipation of food stores for the winter and seed crops for the spring. We were so endeared to some of those trees, that we would map their location and keep yearly logs on their successes or failures at providing us with a harvest. These trees included apples, persimmons, paw paws, mulberries, hickories, beech, oaks, black walnut, butternut, and even ginko.

It wasn't until the Fall of 1982, the year that I first met Annie, that I tasted my first chestnut. That Fall, we were both introduced to these tasty and nutritious treats by our friend and fellow classmate, Hill Craddock. We spent the afternoon gathering chestnuts under some local trees, loaded down our bikes with our harvest, and headed home for a meal. Hill also taught Annie and I how to roast our first chestnuts on the stove top in an iron skillet. We were instantly infected with the sweet aroma and wonderful flavor of roasting chestnuts, but had no idea then that chestnuts would become such an important part of our lives, eventually becoming a seasonal staple in our diet.

Since that memorable day, Annie and I have included chestnut trees in our Fall nut forays, and have not missed a single harvest. In fact, Annie and I now spend most of our Fall energy with gathering and marketing chestnuts. We have since settled in the Pacific Northwest, and did so primarily to raise chestnuts commercially. Here we can grow chestnut trees to record size, thereby utilizing them for timber as well. Our orchard trees are just starting to produce their first crops.

The record of chestnut culture dates over 6000 years. Many cultures, from China to North America, have discovered the wholesomeness and diversity of chestnuts. This cookbook represents some of the meals from these cultures. Included also is basic storage, processing, and nutritional information which may be useful for anyone interested in preparing chestnuts. This book is only a guide, intended to cultivate your interest in chestnuts, as well as whet your appetite for the most diverse nut in the culinary world. Please use your imagination and enjoy participating in the romance of a cuisine that is shared worldwide.

Omroa Bhagwandin,
Onalaska, WA
October 1, 1995

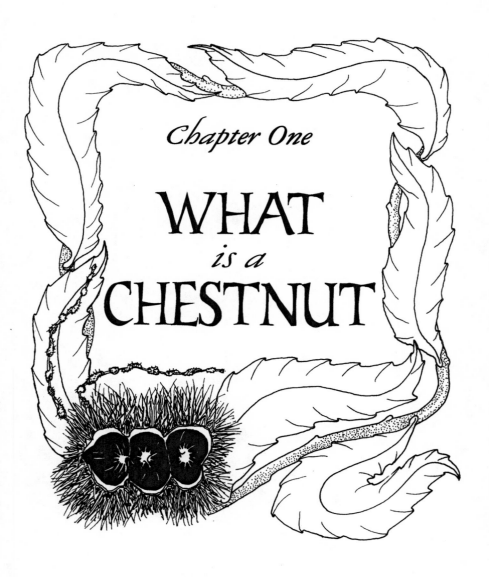

Chapter One

WHAT
is a
CHESTNUT

Castanea spp.

The question, "What is a chestnut?", is commonly asked. This question usually evolves into a discussion of what is *not* a chestnut. The horsechestnut, *(Aesculus hippocastanum)*, and its cousin the buckeye, are often confused with the edible chestnut. It is a common landscape tree known for its showy flowers which bloom in early Spring. An easy way to tell the difference between the horsechestnut and the edible chestnut is by the leaf shape. The horsechestnut has a palmatly compound leaf with five to seven leaflets radiating from the center of the leaf. The edible sweet chestnut has a simple leaf that is oblong and lance shaped, forming a point at the top.

Why the tree is called a horsechestnut is somewhat speculative. The term "horse", in a botanical sense, doesn't necessarily refer to the mammal, but rather, to a characteristic of being large or coarse. The nuts are

Aesculus hippocastanum

extremely bitter and therefore considered inedible and even poisonous. These nuts are well known by English children and are utilized in the game of "Conkers" (originally "Conquerors"), where the nuts are attached to either end of a stout string and swung about. Longfellow's "spreading chestnut tree", from the poem *The Village Blacksmith*, was a horsechestnut.

The water chestnut, *(Eleocharis dulcis)*, used in many oriental dishes, is not a true chestnut either. It is the starchy edible corm of a Chinese water sedge. Water chestnuts are commercially cultivated in the warm climates of Asian countries. When asking for canned chestnuts, most American grocers are sure to lead you to the waterchestnut.

Eleocharis dulcis

The chestnut referred to in this cookbook is the sweet tasting, edible, large, brown, starchy seed (or nut) of the chestnut tree, (*Castanea spp.*). In *Trees Worth Knowing*, the edible chestnut is aptly described by Julia Rogers as follows: "The nut of this tree is hung high aloft, wrapped in a silk wrapper, which is enclosed in a case of sole leather, which again is packed in a mass of shock absorbing, vermin proof pulp, sealed up in a waterproof, ironwood case, and finally cased in a vegetable porcupine of spines, almost impregnable. There is no nut so protected; there is no nut in our woods to compare with it as food."

Chestnuts have been part of the human diet for at least 6000 years. They have kept whole nations from starvation in times of war and have titilated the palettes of nobility over the ages. These huge spreading trees cover the hills of many continents, with native species represented in Europe, China, Japan, and America. Because of its rot resistance and high tensile strength, the people of these lands use the wood for a variety of uses including shingles, beams, fence and trellis posts, siding, furniture manufacture, crates, in ship building and charcoal production. Chestnut wood and bark has also traditionally been an important source of tannic acid.

Chestnut leaves have been used medicinally as an aid for throat pain, excess mucus and as a disinfectant. The leaves are also used for stable bedding and are further recycled into fertilizer for the orchard. A rinse made from chestnut shells is claimed to restore hair growth. The nuts are used not only for human consumption, but for fattening livestock and as a wildlife forage.

Box of chestnut leaves sold as medicine, circa 1900's

The native American chestnut population has declined to near extinction due to a fungal blight, *(Cryphonectria parasitica)*, introduced from Asia in the early 1900's. At one time nearly one out of every four trees in the deciduous forests of the Eastern United States was a chestnut tree. Of those 3.5 billion trees, all that survive today are a few isolated stands of uninfected trees, and the stump sprouts of blighted trees.

There are several organizations and dedicated individuals working to restore the American chestnut to its former glory in the United States, the most prominent of which is The American Chestnut Foundation. At their Wagner Research farm in Meadowview, Virginia, they have been breeding blight resistance into the American chestnut, and due to their efforts, it is conceivable that in the not to distant future, blight resistant American chestnut trees will begin to cover the landscape. This would greatly enhance regional deciduous forest ecology.

Chestnut also played an important part in the economy of Colonial America, being utilized in the charcoal, tannin and the in-shell nut industries. It was also an important part of the culture of the Native American peoples and represented a critical component of the diet of a diversity of forest fauna.

The Iroquois nation realized this importance and celebrated the chestnut tree's gift of sustenance with the magical tale of *Hodadenon and the Chestnut Tree*. In this story, the young boy Hodadenon, which means "The Last One Left", lives alone with his uncle. All of his relations have been killed by a group of seven evil witches. These witches hold a magnificent grove of chestnut trees in their power, not sharing even one nut with the tiniest of creatures. In fact, these evil witches had even enslaved and enchanted rattlesnakes, great bears and panthers, forcing them to guard the chestnut grove.

As the story goes, Hodadenon foolishly destroys the last bit of his uncle's cache of dried chestnuts, thereby precipitating his uncle's eminent doom, as his uncle can eat nothing but chestnuts. The young Hodadenon resolves to brave a venture to the evil witches' guarded grove of chestnuts and steal some of the nuts for his uncle.

Hodadenon cleverly frees the sentinels from the evil ones' spell and thus gains access to the chestnut grove. By finally destroying the seven greedy witches, he breaks their wicked curse. The bones of all his relations, which were scattered upon the ground, magically return to life. Before Hodadenon appear his parents, brothers and sisters, cousins, aunts and uncles and even his grandparents. He gives each of his relations chestnuts and instructs them to plant the seeds everywhere. As the story ends, Hodadenon declares that chestnuts are a sacred food, to be shared with everyone, forever after.

The chestnut was and still is a substantial factor of the lives and economy of the chestnut growing regions of Europe. Throughout history the chestnut forests and orchards have kept the people alive during times of war and famine.

The following story was told to my husband by a chestnut farmer from Northern Italy, Sig. Salarin, who recounted how his family's orchards and the local chestnut forests were changed as a result of World War II.

To be a male in northern Italy meant sure death if found by Nazi soldiers, therefore the menfolk were forced into hiding in the woods. When the soldiers came they pillaged all the farm animals for their own use. They even took produce from the gardens and left the farm families starving. The women were sometimes forced to reveal the whereabouts of their men, but most resisted. They would sneak away at dark and leave food at a predetermined sight for the men hiding in the woods. For years this went on, and often the only food available were the chestnuts and wild mushrooms that were abundant in the forests.

After the war, all were left destitute. There was nothing left but the huge ancient forest of chestnut. They brought down these megolyths with two man handsaws and sometimes dynomite to blast the six meter diameter trunks into sizes which could be managed onto the mule carts. The wood was taken to the cities and sold for tannin.

With the tannin money they bought another cow and a few chickens in order to start over. All that was left of the vast hillsides were chestnut stumps, but these trees had literally saved their lives. Something that may have seemed a bit like magic happened the following Spring. The roots of those venerable old trees sent up vigorous green sprouts.

The WORLD *of*

C. dentata (N. America)

NATIVE RANGE ▦

Anglo Saxon - Cistel

Old English - Chesten

German - Kastanie

Spanish - Castaña

French - Chataigne or Marron

Italian - Castagne or Marrone

CHESTNUTS

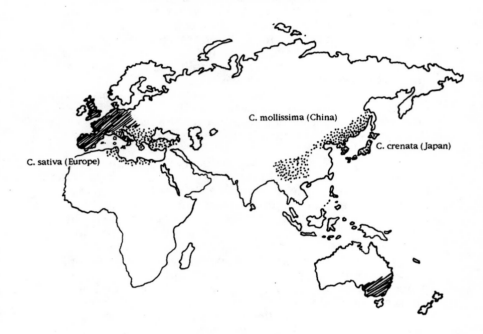

C. mollissima (China)

C. crenata (Japan)

C. sativa (Europe)

INTRODUCED CULTIVATION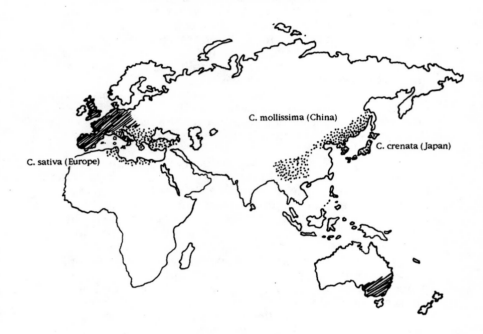

Eastern Native American - O-heh-yah-tah

Greek - Kastana

Japanese - Kuri

Chinese - Lee shu

Russian - Kashtan

Galic - Ganmchro

15

Growing chestnut trees is fairly simple and can be quite rewarding. As little as two trees is all that is needed to produce enough chestnuts for the average household.

Chestnuts flower during early Summer, and thus escape any threat of frost, although in rare years pollination can be adversly affected by heavy rains. Male and female flowers occur on the same tree, but a chestnut tree's pollen is generally self sterile, except in a few isolated cases. This means that a chestnut tree can not pollinate itself and make nuts. There must be at least two genetically distinct varieties or separate seedlings for cross pollination. Pollen is born on catkins and pollination is effected thru wind dispersal and, to a limited extent, with the aid of insects (bees will work chestnuts). Nuts begin to ripen in early Autumn.

Chestnuts are prolific nut producers with annual yields averaging 250-300 lbs. (110-135 kg) per mature tree. Start looking for the first nuts from a newly planted tree in the 4th to 7th year from seedling trees, and half again as early from grafted trees. Grafted trees have an advantage in that they will produce nuts earlier in the life of the tree and will produce a nut of known characteristics, although the trees are much more expensive and less vigorous as young trees than seedling trees. For a grafted orchard, with the proper variety on a good site, expected yeilds should be in the range of 10 lbs. (4.5 kg) /tree in the 10th - 12th year from establishment. If allowed to harden off successfully, chestnut trees should be able to withstand winter temperatures of up to -25F (-30C).

Site selection is important for the success of a chestnut orchard. Although chestnuts are relatively hardy, buds will tend to break dormancy early in the spring and can be susceptible to late frosts. For this reason it is wise to plant chestnuts on sloping ground with good air drainage.

Chestnuts will tolerate a wide variety of soils, generally prefering a deep, sandy loam. The most critical factor for soils compatible for chestnuts is that the soil must be slightly acidic and well drained. Chestnuts should not be allowed to have their roots in standing water, as they are prone to root rot. Locating an orchard on sloping ground will help alleviate soil drainage problems. Irrigation the first several years during establishment is essential. During nut ripening, properly timed watering has been shown to increase nut size and yield of chestnuts, although they are generally considered to be drought tolerant once established.

Chapter Two

HARVEST TIME

The chestnut tree is praised for its beauty, especially in early Summer when the golden catkin flowers appear to burst forth like fireworks. In early Autumn the nuts begin to ripen and fall. These nuts are held tight within large green burrs which are not much different in appearance than sea urchins. When ripe, these burrs will open on the tree, yielding an abundance of rich "chestnut brown" nuts, which then fall free from the burrs. Some chestnut trees will drop unopened burrs with nuts still enclosed. These burrs can be harvested and when allowed to dry out will open up to reveal the nuts inside. Once the nuts are ripe they begin to fall a little every day, but generally drop in several large flushes, due to strong winds.

Those who plan on collecting chestnuts should equip themselves with a couple of plastic buckets, a pair of latex gloves which give good finger control but are thick enough to resist chestnut-burr spines, a wide tined rake and several clean plastic mesh bags (large onion sacks). Having the grass mowed short under the canopy of the chestnut trees, prior to the nut fall, will make gathering much easier.

It is best to gather chestnuts daily to prevent the nuts from being dried out or consumed by wildlife. Begin by shaking any trees or limbs that are still small enough to shake. Many ripe nuts, which the wind hasn't rattled loose, will tumble down. All that's left to do is simply gather these up by hand and put them in the buckets.

Harvesting chestnuts after the leaves have fallen involves a bit more work but, can be done with the help of a rake. Begin at the outer canopy of the tree, rake a circular row around and away from the base of the tree. Rake back the

leaves and burrs to expose the chestnuts. Continue this process in concentric rings around the tree until all of the nuts are collected. You should go back to the raked up rows of leaves and burrs to search for nuts that are still enclosed in unopened burrs. These nuts will pop out by stepping on the edge of the burrs. You will also find some nuts that had been raked up along with the burr and leaf litter.

One can usually pick about 20 pounds (9 kg) an hour. A day of picking can easily yield 100 pounds (45 kg) of chestnuts. This is enough for about 70 meals (at four servings per meal), which is a good store for a family of four.

Chestnuts are perishable, therefore, special care should be taken in their cleaning and storage. Chestnuts should be cleaned immediately after harvesting. Surface dirt, which contains mold spores, needs to be removed. Any rotten and split shelled nuts should be sorted out. The culls that have split shells and are not rotten may be eaten right away or, can be frozen in-shell for later use.

One method for cleaning the nuts is by buffing them. This can be done by taking an old shrunken wool blanket and sewing up two sides to make a sack. Place about 15 pounds (7 kg) of chestnuts in the sack. Close the open end and rub and shake the nuts around in the sack for a few minutes. The nuts will come out shiny and clean. Another way to clean the nuts is by washing them in a large tub or sink full of cool water with a concentration of 1% chlorine bleach. This will sanitize the surface of the nuts but may dull their shells a bit.

Nuts with worms can be cleaned by dipping the contaminated chestnuts in a 122 F (50 C) water bath for 45 minutes immediately followed by a dip into near freezing water to quickly cool the nuts. This process heats the nuts enough to kill the larvae, yet not so hot to kill the germ of the nut. The heat also activates the nuts to begin germinating, which is why they must be quickly cooled. Any wet nuts needto be surface dried before storage.

The ideal storage temperature for chestnuts is around 32 degrees F (0C) and about 85% relative humidity. Nuts stored in paper or plastic bags do not keep well. This is because the storage container needs to allow for the chestnuts to "breathe". Chestnuts can be stored in onion sacks in a well ventilated part of the garage or basement for about a month.

For long term storage of fresh chestnuts, layer nuts in clean dry sawdust, sand, or peat moss into plastic buckets with tight fitting lids. Keep the lids off for the first few days to allow any condensation from the nuts to dry off. Once sealed, these will keep nearly a year in the fruit cellar. Check periodically for any moldy nuts and repack.

The process of curing chestnuts converts some of the starches to sugars which improves their flavor. This can be done by spreading them out out in a fairly warm area, (not to exceed 85 degrees F (29C)), for 2-5 days. The nuts will lose about 10% of their field weight. Nuts that loose any more than 20% of their field weight will have a tendency to mold quickly. Cured nuts should just start to lose their firmness. Squeeze the nuts to test, and any sizable air gap between the shell and the nutmeat indicates overdrying.

Freezing chestnuts in the shell is quite simple and nuts will keep for up to a year this way. Place clean raw chestnuts in plastic bags and seal tight. Thaw only the amount needed and process as if they were fresh. Once the nuts are thawed they need to be kept refrigerated and will only keep a few days before spoiling.

For centuries European peasantry have put up a good supply of chestnuts every year by drying them. A good size barn, usually made of stone, with two stories, is employed. The process is as follows: The nuts are spread about a foot deep on the second floor and a slow fire of chestnut logs and sawdust burns on the main floor. The heat and smoke rise through the cracks of the second floor, drying the nuts, while the smoke escapes between the roof tiles. This goes on until the nuts are rock hard. The heat and smoke drives out any larvae, which drop down to anxiously waiting barnyard fowl.

In more ancient times the dried chestnuts were peeled by stomping on them with spiked-soled shoes. Today an ingenious contraption much like a tractor driven bean sheller sits under the exit shoot of the drying sheds and shells the nuts as they are scooped off the drying racks into the shelling hopper below. The nuts and shells are separated and the yellow kernals are left to be stored in air tight containers in the pantry.

To dry nuts at home, try putting them on a tray in the oven at a low temperature while leaving the door ajar; or in a conventional food dryer. Some folks could build a special rack right above the wood stove and maintain a slow fire. Once the nuts are dried they can be peeled by putting them in gunnysacks and beat on a hard floor or with a hammer until the shell cracks and abraids off inside the sack. I've seen two men grab the ends of the sack and beat it against a tree trunk or brick wall. The chestnut shells are brittle and will break up fairly easily. Once this is done the nuts need to be separated from the shells and stored in a cool air tight, bug and vermin proof container. Nuts preserved this way can keep well for several years.

Chestnut flour can be made by grinding dried nuts and is used in many ways. If drying nuts for flour, the nuts should be cut into quarters prior to drying, or broken into pieces with a hammer after drying. Either way, the dried nuts need to be a size the mill can accept.

For those who do not have their own chestnut trees to pick from, look for chestnuts at the grocers or farmer's markets in late Fall. In selecting nuts, be certain that they are of good color and feel firm. Check for visible signs of mold. Chestnuts that are darker than the others or have a sour smell are most generally bad, and should not be purchased.

The local crop will always be the freshest but should still be checked for other qualities. Peel back the shell with a pocket knife or fingernail and see how easily the pellicle (inner peel) comes off. Go ahead and taste the nut. Is it sweet? Does the pellicle have an overly offensive taste? If the pellicle is edible, then how easily it peels is of little importance. Nuts that are very convoluted, (when the pellicle grows into the nut meat), with bitter tasting pellicles, are not usually worth the time peeling, unless they are very large.

Each individual tree varies in nut quality as to size, flavor, and peelability. If you like what you have found, then buy enough for at least a few recipes, as well as for roasting. Chances are the supply could be gone when you go back for more. A few pounds will keep in a mesh bag in the the lettuce drawer of the refrigerator for as long as two months.

However you go about procuring your stash of chestnuts, remember to treat them more like a fresh vegetable, rather than a nut, when considering proper storage.

CHESTNUT NUTRITION

The composition of chestnuts is much different than any other nut. Folk names such as "bread of the mountains", "nut grain" and "corn tree" helps one to begin to understand this difference. Consisting primarily of carbohydrates and water with virtually no fats to speak of, chestnuts act more like a grain than a nut. Grinding dried chestnuts result in a fine sweet flour rather than a nut butter as with almonds or hazelnuts.

This unique composition is the basis for its culinary diversity. Fresh chestnuts can be prepared as a vegetable (similar to potatoes). They can also be mashed to form a purée and served savory or sweet allowing them to be the focus of any course of the meal including confections and desserts. Chestnut flour likewise can be used to thicken and flavor soups, sauces and gravies as well as add flavor to pastas and pastries.

Although chestnuts only contain 4% protein by weight, it is a complete protein containing 13 amino acids, 8 of which are considered essential. Chestnuts are a healthy source of nutrition and are promoted as a low fat food by the American Heart Association. Eat them and enjoy good health!

Approximate composition of one cup (150g) peeled fresh chestnuts:

Calories............................ 285
Protein .... 6.3 g
Fat ....1.7 g
Carbohydrates...........74 g
Water............................. 66 g
Fiber ....2.6 g

VITAMINS

B1 .... 0.35 mg
B2 .... 0.35 mg
B6 .... 0.53 mg
B12 .... 0.0 mg
Niacin .... 1.0 mg
B5 .... 0.76 mg
C .... 9.6 mg
E .... 0.8 mg

MINERALS

Sodium ....:4.5 mg
Phosphorus 144 mg
Potassium ... 670 mg
Calcium .... 27 mg
Iron .... 2.1 mg
Magnesium .. 126 mg
Copper .... 0.5 mg
Manganese .... 2.4 mg
Zinc ....1.4 mg

Equivalents which you may find useful:

28 fresh chestnuts in-shell (average) = **1 lb. (450 grams)**

1 lb. **(450 grams)** fresh chestnuts in-shell = **3 cups (425 grams)**
of peeled nut meats

3 cups (425 grams) of peeled nut meats = **1 cup (175 grams)**
chestnut flour

1 1/4 lb. (560 grams) of fresh chestnuts in-shell = **2 cups (475 grams)**
of chestnut purée

1 lb. (450 grams) dried peeled chestnuts = **1 3/4 lbs. (800 grams)**
4 cups after rehydration

Allow about **1/3 lb. (150 grams)** of fresh chestnuts per serving.

Many folks say chestnuts are too much of a bother to peel. Perhaps they just don't realize there is a trick to it. Almost all recipes call for the nuts to be peeled first. The way they are to be used in the recipe will determine the best method for peeling.

ROASTED CHESTNUTS

Nuts to be used whole or in large pieces can be roasted. To roast a chestnut, you must first pierce the shell to allow hot air to escape while cooking. Use a sharp paring knife to cut a slash or an X through the shell, but not into the meat.The larger of a cut that is made the easier the nut will be to peel. Once this is done to the nuts, all sides must then be heated thoroughly.When the nuts are roasted, the shell will begin to curl away from the cut. The meat will be yellow, soft, and smell sweet. In a chestnut pan or a dry skillet, roast the chestnuts by shaking in or over a medium heat for about 20 minutes. In the microwave oven, place a dozen chestnuts around the outer edge of a paper plate and cook on "high" for four minutes. In the oven, place the chestnuts on a cookie sheet or cake pan, sprinkle generously with water, and bake at 400 F (200C/gas 6) for 15 to 20 minutes. The nuts come out firmer when baked.

Whatever method you choose to roast chestnuts, be certain to slice the shell first and to peel them while they are still hot. Hot roasted chestnuts are an all time favorite, especially with children!

Chestnut roasting pan

PEELING CHESTNUTS

The easiest way to peel chestnuts for most recipes is by boiling. Cut the supply of chestnuts in half from top to bottom as shown.

Discard any that look dark brown inside or smell offensive. Place the nuts in a deep pot with just enough water to cover them. Cover and boil for 5 minutes. Scoop out a few nuts with a slotted spoon and as soon as they are just cool enough to handle, but still very hot, pop the nuts out of their skins. If they don't pop from the pellicles very easily, they are either too cool, or not cooked enough. With nuts that are too cool, simply throw them back into the pot, stir them down to the bottom, and try another spoonfull. If they are not cooked enough, change the water and boil another 5 minutes.

Chestnut knife

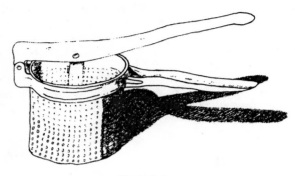

Chestnut ricer

PURÉE

Many recipes call for puree or meal. To make purée, boil the nuts and peel as described above. After all the chestnuts are peeled, boil another 10 minutes in a smaller amount of fresh water, broth, or milk, depending on the recipe. Use a food processor, potato masher, or chestnut ricer to make a smooth paste. Purée can also be made from dried nuts, soaked overnight, and then boiled until very soft. The consistency of the purée can vary, from a thick paste to a creamy batter. This is dependent on how much liquid is added while processing. A perfect purée is about as thick as softened butter. It wild hold its shape until a knife is taken to it. For those less adventuresome, purée is sold in cans, either sweetened, or 'au naturel', and require only a can opener.

DRIED, PEELED CHESTNUTS

Dried and already peeled chestnuts need only to be rehydrated, the same as dried beans, before using. For tenacious pellicles, place the dried nuts in very hot water for a few minutes before soaking. The pellicle will expand before the nut does and will then come off easily with your fingers under a gentle spray of warm water.

For recipes calling for a half pound (225 g), or about 2 cups, place the nuts in an enamel or glass pot large enough to allow the nuts to swell. Pour three cups (750 ml) boiling water over the nuts, cover and set aside for 15 to 20 minutes. Pull off any brown pellicle which will have loosened from the nuts and set the pot to simmer on a low heat until the nuts are tender. This should take about 2 hours. Add more water if the nuts get dry during cooking. Some recipes will call for the nuts to simmer in broth or milk. In this case, after soaking the nuts in hot water, pour off the water and simmer in the broth or milk.

Dried nuts can also be rehydrated by soaking in water, in the refrgerator, overnight. These nuts can then be boiled or placed raw in a stuffing.

CHESTNUT FLOUR

Chestnut flour first became popular in Europe during the Middle Ages. It can be found in most specialty food stores. Be wary of flour which contains little brown specs, this means the pellicle was ground with the nut. Flour of this type is of a lesser quality and will not have such a pleasant taste. Imported chestnut flour may often have a bitter or smokey flavor due to its age and processing. This can be overcome by spreading the flour on a cookie sheet and lightly roasting it in a cool oven, (150 F, 65 C or gas 1/4), for a few minutes. Watch it carefully and do not allow the flour to brown. Grind your own flour from dried chestnuts with any flour mill. The finer the flour is ground, the finer the cooked product will be. Chestnut flour can be used to thicken soups, make quick sauces and gravies, or in any breads, cakes, puddings, or pastas.

Gluten, the substance in wheat flour that allows breads and cakes to rise, is not present in chestnut flour. Therefore, most traditional chestnut breads and cakes are flat. A general rule for using chestnut flour in lighter cakes and bread recipes, is to use no more that one third chestnut flour to wheat flour.

Chapter Three

SOUPS
and
SAUCES

pples and chestnuts seem to have a culinary symbiotic relationship which, like true lovers, compliment, enhance and enrich each other. Any culture that has access to chestnuts and apples will inevitably serve them in a dish together, be it hot mulled cider and roasted chestnuts, braised and served with game, in a salad, or even in soup. What follows are two soup recipes of French origin.

POTAGE PURÉE DE MARRONS

FRANCE   SERVES 4

2 cups (475 g) chestnut purée

4 cups (1 liter) chicken or vegetable broth

1/4 cup (60 ml) Madiera or Burgundy

1 large tart apple

2 Tablespoons (25 g) butter

Simmer the chestnut purée with the broth and wine for a short time. Sauté thin slices of apple in butter until soft. Laddle soup into bowls and lay apple slices on top. Garnish with fresh peppergrass or watercress.

CHESTNUT AND APPLE SOUP

FRANCE   SERVES 4

This recipe may be preferred by the younger folk.

2 cups (475 g) chestnut purée

4 cups (1 liter) chicken or vegetable broth

2 apples

2 Tablespoons (25 g) butter

1/4 cup (60 ml) very hot milk

Cook the purée with the broth. Slice the apples and sauté in butter until soft. Purée the apples in an electric blender and add to the soup. Stir in hot milk and serve. Garnish with a dash of paprika and seasoned croutons.

DUTCH CHESTNUT SOUP

HOLLAND   SERVES 4

This is a hearty course on its own and is quite satisfying served with thick wedges of hot buttered rye bread.

1 large onion (finely chopped)

2 stalks celery (finely chopped)

1 lb. (450 g) seasoned pork sausage

4 cups (1 liter) water or stock

2 cups (475 g) chestnut purée

1 cup (250 g) mashed cooked lentils

1/4 cup (30 g) arrowroot powder

1/2 cup (120 ml.) cream

2 large sprigs fresh parsley (minced)

Sauté onion, celery and chopped sausage in a soup pot until the meat is browned. Add water (or stock), chestnut purée and mashed lentils. Cook for 20 minutes. Mix the arrowroot powder into the cream quite well (no lumps), then stir this mixture in with the soup. Cook another 10 or 15 minutes or until thick, stirring occasionally. Garnish with the parsley and serve.

The fate of a recipe lies in the hand of the almighty creator - the cook. In search of chestnut recipes, I found several references to a soup of apparent English origin (that is, as far back as I can trace). This soup combines many meats and herbal seasonings to create a thick, hearty broth with whole chestnuts and pigeons. The following recipe was originally printed in The Art of Cookery Made Plain and Simple, 1747 by Mrs. Hannah Glass, appears in a 1783 publication, again in 1797 and ever so often up to today and always slightly modified to accomodate current culinary trends. Here is the recipe word for word, from John Farley, 1783 and the recipe again 152 years later from Mrs. Chell of Essex, 1935.

CHESTNUT SOUP

ENGLAND   SERVES: 1 HUNGRY TRAVELER

Pick half a hundred of chestnuts, put them in an earthen pan, and put them in the oven for half an hour, or roast them gently over a slow fire; but take care they do not burn. Then peel them, and set them to stew in a quart of good beef, veal, or mutton broth, till they be quite tender. In the mean time, take a piece or slice of ham or bacon, a pound of veal, a pigeon beat to pieces, an onion, a bundle of sweet herbs, a piece of carrot, and a little pepper and mace. Lay the bacon at the bottom of a stew pan, and lay the meat and ingredients on it. Set it over a slow fire till it begins to stick to the pan, and then put in a crust of bread, and pour in 2 quarts of broth. Let it boil softly till one third be wasted, then strain it off, and put in the chestnuts. Season it with salt, and let boil till it be well tasted. Then stew 2 pigeons in it, and a french roll fried crisp. Lay the roll in the middle of the dish and the pigeons on each side; pour in the soup and send it up hot.

CHESTNUT SOUP

ENGLAND   SERVES: 6

This is a much simpler version of the previous soup, to be sure! Cream could be substituted for the milk. With the addition of a half teaspoon of nutmeg and a pinch of cayenne, yet another variation of this vintage soup is created, and is often served to cold yuletide guests and holiday carollers.

2 cups (475 g) chestnut purée

4 cups (1 liter) chicken stock

2 cups (475 ml) milk

1 pinch mace

salt and pepper to taste

Mix the chestnut purée in a saucepan with the stock, milk and mace. Heat and season to taste with salt and pepper. Serve hot.

MINESTRONE DI CASTAGNE

ITALY   SERVES: 6

This soup was prepared and served to my husband and I by Sig. Diego Decorte in the Piedmont region of Italy where he says chestnuts are always cooked with bay. The recipe, passed down from his mother, calls for pork rind, "for flavor and for the ones working 12 hours with a hoe in the hills". This recipe is perfect for an electric crockpot and should be cooked in a ceramic pot, none the less.

1 onion

1 pretty carrot

2 celery stalks

2 Tablespoons olive oil

1 ham hock

1 1/2 cups (300 g) fresh or rehydrated dry *Scarlet Runner* beans

4 medium potatoes

2 lbs. (900 g) fresh chestnuts

6 cups (1 1/2 liters) hot water

4 or 5 bay leaves

1/2 of a hot pepper

olive oil

grated *Parmesan* cheese

Chop up and sauté the vegetables in the olive oil. Add the ham hock and brown. Wash beans, wash and chop up potatoes and roast and peel chestnuts (see page 25). Add all this, and the hot water to the pot. Add bay and hot pepper. Bring to a boil and cook for at least 2 1/2 hours. Serve with a dribble of *extra virgin* olive oil and a sprinkle of *Parmesan* cheese.

MINESTRA DI CASTAGNE

ITALY   SERVES: 6

*T*his is a lighter soup and is quite different from the previous recipe.

35 fresh or dried peeled chestnuts

1 small onion (whole)

1 stalk celery (cut in half)

1 small carrot (whole)

4 cups (1 liter) milk

2 cups (475 ml) water

1/8 teaspoon nutmeg

salt and pepper to taste

1/2 cup (100 g) uncooked rice

Peel chestnuts by boiling (see page 26), or prepare the dried, peeled chestnuts (see page 27). Simmer the chestnuts, onion, celery, carrot, milk, water and spices in a covered soup pot for 1 hour. Remove the vegetables from the soup and discard. Add the rice. Add more hot liquid if necessary. Cook rice until tender and serve.

HUNGARIAN CHESTNUT SOUP

HUNGARY   SERVES: 4

The ingredients in this soup, though quite traditional, amount to a high cholesterol meal. The butter may be replaced with olive oil and the pork can be a lean cut. The whipping cream may be replaced with light cream.

36 chestnuts

1/4 cup (50 g) butter

1/2 lb. (225 g) pork

1 medium size parsnip

1 large carrot

3 stalks celery

2 teaspoons paprika

4 cups (1 liter) chicken broth

1 cup (250 ml) whipping cream

3 egg yolks

salt and pepper to taste

Roast and peel chestnuts (see page 25), or use dried, peeled chestnuts which have been soaked over night. Chop fine in food processor and set aside. Melt butter in heavy soup pot. Chop the pork into cubes and brown in the butter. Chop the parsnip, carrot and celery and add to the pot. Stir this and let cook until the vegetables are tender. Do not let it burn. Add the chestnuts and paprika, and then add the broth. Simmer until the flavors are well blended and all is quite tender, at least 30 minutes. Beat cream and yolks in a small bowl. Whisk a cup of cooled soup into the mixture and then stir the cream mixture into the soup. Lower the heat and stir until thick; do not let it boil at this point. Season with salt and pepper and garnish each bowl with a sprinkle of paprika.

RUSSIAN SOUP

FORMER SOVIET UNION   SERVES: 6-8

This soup is similar to the Hungarian soup recipe, yet with much less of the cholesterol and thus, a bit lighter fare. If veal stock is not to be had, a beef broth will do. The cinnamon gives this soup a pleasant glow.

28 fresh chestnuts

6 cups (1 1/2 liters) stock

1 celery stalk

salt and pepper to taste

1 egg yolk

1 cup (250 ml) milk

2 teaspoons cinnamon

Roast or boil and peel the chestnuts, (see pages 25-26). In a heavy pot add the stock, chestnuts, celery, salt and pepper. Cover and let simmer for well over an hour. Remove the celery and discard. Blend the soup in an electric mixer until smooth, then return it to the pot. Blend egg yolk and milk together and slowly whisk into the soup. Do not let it boil. Add cinnamon, stir and serve. Sprinkle a pinch of cinnamon on top as a garnish.

Drying barn, for drying chestnuts. Europe

CHINESE WINTER SOUP

WESTERN CHINA   SERVES: 6

Though called a winter soup, it could be served anytime of the year. In the Spring, add pea greens or snow peas shortly before serving.

1 lb. (450 g) tofu or salt pork

2 Tablespoons peanut oil

1 small pod red chili pepper

1/4 lb. (110 g) *Shiitake* mushrooms

6 cups (1 1/2 liters) water

28 chestnuts

2 medium parsnips

2 medium turnips

2 leeks

1 small winter squash

1 Tablespoon vinegar

soy sauce to taste

2 Tablespoons fresh cilantro

Chop the tofu or pork into squares and brown in peanut oil in the bottom of a soup pot. Cut the chili pepper in half lengthwise and remove the seeds. Add the pepper to the pot. Slice the mushrooms and sauté everything together until soft. Add the water and bring to a boil. If using fresh chestnuts, have them roasted and peeled before hand, (see page 25). Dried peeled chestnuts can be used, but must be soaked overnight. Add the chestnuts to the soup. Chop the parsnips, turnips and leeks and add to the soup. Peel, seed and chop the winter squash into bite size squares and add to the pot, then add the vinegar. Cook until the vegetables are just tender. Add soysauce to taste and finely chopped cilantro. Serve with noodles or steamed Chinese buns.

COLONIAL STYLE CHESTNUT SAUCE

COLONIAL AMERICA   SERVES: 4

*W*ith the help of the friendly natives, the early colonists soon discovered sweet American chestnuts and were no doubt glad to find them similar, if not better than, chestnuts from the motherland. The abundance of these chestnuts in the Eastern forests was a factor in creating a strong local economy and thus, eventually the strength to be truly independent. Although American chestnuts are now scarce, any available fresh chestnuts will do just fine.

1 lb. (450 g) fresh chestnuts or 1 1/2 cups (350 g) unsweetened chestnut purée	Peel the chestnuts by boiling, (see page 26) and cook them in the stock until tender. The stock will be greatly reduced in the process. Press through a sieve or use a blender to make a purée and return it to the pot. If using unsweetened canned purée, use only 1 cup of stock and heat thoroughly. Add butter and stir until melted. Add cream slowly while stirring; add enough for desired consistency. Season and serve over vegetables and/or fowl.
3 cups (750 ml) stock	
1/2 cup (110 g) butter	
1 cup (250 ml) cream	
salt and pepper to taste	

*A*nother version found in *The New England Cookbook* creates basically the same sauce as the Colonial Style Sauce above, but before serving add one pound of fried and drained, ground pork sausage. A darker sauce will be had if the sausage has a chance to simmer in the sauce for a while. As a young girl in central Ohio, I was served this sauce over toast. It was a meal I remember, even to this day, as quite gratifying.

A third variation of this sauce served by chef W. G. Wigglesworth at the Quiet Trails Retreat in Cynthiana, Kentucky, calls for sour cream or yogurt in place of cream and an addition of paprika to be served over potatoes, rice or noodles.

WHITE CREAM SAUCE

SOUTHERN EUROPE   SERVES: 6

An excellent sauce which can be served anytime of the year, especially when fresh chestnuts are not to be had. Smother lightly steamed Spring vegetables or seafood and fettuccine with this aromatic sauce.

2 shallots or 1 small onion

1/2 cup (110 g) butter

1 sprig of rosemary

1/4 cup (45 g) chestnut flour sifted

1/4 cup (30 g) arrowroot powder

1 cup (250 ml) water

2 cups (475 ml) milk

salt and white pepper

Peel and cut in half the shallots or onion. Melt the butter in a shallow sauce pan. Add the shallots and rosemary. Simmer slowly until the butter is saturated with the flavors of shallot and rosemary. Remove these from the butter. Whisk in the chestnut flour and then the arrowroot powder. Whisk smooth and simmer 3-5 minutes. Slowly add water while whisking and then add the milk. Season with salt and pepper.

CHESTNUT BROWN SAUCE

EUROPE   SERVES: 6

Add to a basic brown gravy coarsely chopped chestnuts and there you have it. A fine gravy for any game, including fowl.

3/4 lb. (350 g) fresh chestnuts

1/4 cup (50 g) drippings or butter

2 Tablespoons grated onion

2 Tablespoons grated carrot

1 bay leaf

4 whole cloves

1/4 cup (35 g) flour

2 cups (475 ml) meat stock

Salt and pepper to taste

Roast and peel chestnuts (see page 25). Chop them coarsely and set aside. Heat butter or drippings in a heavy skillet. Over a low heat simmer the onion, carrot, bay and clove for quite some time, being careful not to let it burn. Slowly add the flour, stirring constantly, Cook until the flour is brown. Remove from heat. Gradually stir in the meat stock. Strain out and discard the vegetables and spices. Return to heat and add chopped chestnuts. Simmer, while stirring, until smooth and thick. Season with salt and pepper and serve.

Chapter Four

SIDE DISHES

GLAZED CHESTNUTS

EUROPE   SERVES: 4

*S*erve on a bed of winter greens as an accompaniment to
any meat dish.

**3/4 lb. (350 g) fresh chestnuts
or 1/2 lb. (225 g) dried, peeled
chestnuts**

2 Tablespoons (25 g) butter

1 Tablespoon honey or sugar

1/2 cup (120 ml) stock

salt and pepper

Lightly roast and peel the
fresh chestnuts or prepare
dried, peeled chestnuts
(see pages 25 or 27). In a
skillet on a low heat melt
the butter and stir in the
honey or sugar. Add the
chestnuts and sauté till
they become light brown.
Add stock and salt and

BRAISED CHESTNUTS

FRANCE   SERVES: 6

*T*o be served with poultry.

**1 1/2 lbs. (700 g) fresh
chestnuts or
3/4 lb. (350 g) dried peeled
chestnuts**

1 onion (quartered)

2 Tablespoons olive oil

1 stalk celery

2 cups (475 ml) chicken broth

1/4 teaspoon allspice

salt and pepper to taste

Lightly roast the chestnuts
and peel them or prepare
dried, peeled chestnuts (see
pages 25 or 27). In an iron
skillet brown the onion in
the oil. Add chestnuts,
celery, broth and spices.
Boil a few minutes, then
cover and braise in an oven
for about 30 minutes. Once
the nuts are tender they are
done.

SAUTÉED CHESTNUTS

NORTHERN EUROPE   SERVES: 6

*S*erve alongside quail or chicken. Add a garnish of
parsley. This dish is also very good without any sauce.

2 lbs. (900 g) fresh chestnuts
or 1 lb. (450 g) dried peeled
chestnuts

3 cloves garlic (or more)

1/4 cup (50 g) butter

3/4 cup (175 ml) heavy cream

Roast chestnuts and peel or
prepare dried peeled
chestnuts (see pages 25 or
27). Mince the garlic and
sauté the chestnuts and
garlic in a skillet over a low
heat until the garlic is
golden. Add cream and
simmer for a few minutes,
stirring gently to cover the
chestnuts.

CHESTNUT PURÉE

GREECE   SERVES: 6

*T*his dish is comparable to mashed potatoes, but only in
texture. The chestnuts give it a slight sweetness and the
broth imparts a bit of heartiness.

2 lbs. (900 g) fresh chestnuts

3 cups (750 ml) chicken broth

1 stalk celery

3 Tablespoons (40 g) butter

salt and pepper

1/2 cup (120 ml) cream

Cut the chestnuts in half
and boil (see page 26). Peel
the nuts while still hot and
cook in a covered pot with
the chicken broth, celery
stalk, butter, salt and
pepper until the nuts are
tender, about 30 minutes.
Remove celery and discard.
Put the nuts through a
ricer, food mill or food
processor with the broth.
Mix in the cream and serve.

46

DEVILED CHESTNUTS

NORTHWESTERN UNITED STATES   SERVES: 6

S ome recently converted chestnut enthusiasts gave me this
recipe. They were munching these tasty snacks at home
while watching the Superbowl playoffs on television.

2 lbs. (900 g) fresh chestnuts

3 Tablespoons butter

Tobasco sauce

Roast and peel the chestnuts
(see page 25). Sauté in
butter until golden.
Sprinkle on the tobasco
sauce to taste.

CAJUN CHESTNUTS

SOUTHEASTERN UNITED STATES   SERVES: 6

Y es, our Mamaw on the Gulf coast keeps her eyes out for
fresh chestnuts in their season, until her newly planted
chestnut trees begin to bear, that is. This is her own recipe,
and it does have a kick!

**1 1/2 lbs. (700 g) fresh
chestnuts**

1 clove garlic

1 Tablespoon butter

1/4 teaspoon sea salt

1 pinch cayenne pepper

1/4 teaspoon chili powder

Roast and peel chestnuts
(see page 25). Mince the
garlic. Sauté the garlic in
the butter for a minute in a
big, heavy skillet. Add the
chestnut and spices and stir
fry for 5 to 7 minutes or
spread in a shallow pan and
roast in a 300 F (150 C or
gas 2) oven until a bit
crispy (about 15-20
minutes).

LENTILS AND CHESTNUTS

ROMAN EMPIRE   SERVES: 6

L entils have been cultivated by humans for quite some time, at least 8000 years or so. Combining them with chestnuts in a meal may date back nearly as far. Garnish with a slice of orange and fresh bay or mint leaves. This dish may be served as a light lunch with a winter salad of cabbage and pickled beans and a slice of nutty brown bread.

1 lb. (450 g) fresh chestnuts or
1/2 lb. (225 g) dried peeled
chestnuts

1 cup (200 g) lentils

4 cups (1 liter) water (or more)

1 Tablespoon honey

2 Tablespoons vinegar

2 Tablespoons olive oil

1/2 teaspoon each of the
following:
chopped parsley
chervil
basil
thyme
mint
ground cumin

1/4 teaspoon each of the
following:
ground pepper
ground corriander

Roast and peel the fresh chestnuts (see page 25) or soak dried chestnuts overnight. Put the chestnuts and washed lentils in a large pot with the water. Cook these together until the chestnuts are tender through and the lentils are cooked. This could take as long as 2 hours. Add water if necessary. If when done cooking there is excess water, drain off all but about 1 cup (250 ml). Add all other ingredients and simmer on low, stirring occasionally for 20 minutes.

GREEK RICE

GREECE   SERVES: 4

*F*ennel has a way of giving foods a lighter taste. Try
serving this dish with the addition of halved and braised
Florence fennel bulbs alongside broiled snapper.

1 cup (200 g) uncooked rice

1/2 lb. (225 g) fresh chestnuts
or 1/4 lb. (110 g) dried peeled
chestnuts

1/4 cup (60 ml) olive oil

1 Tablespoon fennel seed

1/4 cup (50 g) currants or
chopped raisins

salt and pepper

1/2 cup (110 ml) plain yogurt

Cook the rice and meanwhile
roast and peel the chestnuts
or prepare the dried
chestnuts (see pages 25 or
27). Once the rice is
cooked, heat a good sized
skillet and add the olive oil.
To the hot oil add the fennel
seed and chestnuts and
sauté for a few minutes.
Next add the rice and
currants. Mix it all well
then transfer to a serving
dish and fold in the yogurt.
Garnish with fresh fennel
leaves and a lemon wedge.

CHESTNUTS AND RICE

JAPAN   SERVES: 4

*T*his version of rice is traditionally served with fish or seafood. Mirin, a syrupy rice wine, is used as a flavoring and lends an interesting aroma to the dish. Sweetened Japanese chestnuts really must be used and the canned, in heavy syrup, chestnuts from Korea seem to be the best.

1 13 oz. (375 g) can Korean chestnuts in heavy syrup

1 1/2 cups (300 g) uncooked white rice

1 3/4 cups (425 ml) water

2 teaspoons Mirin

gomashio (toasted and ground sesame with salt)

Drain the chestnuts from the syrup and chop into quarters. Save back 2 Tablespoons of the syrup. Wash the rice and drain. In medium sized pot with a tight fitting lid, add the rice, water, reserved syrup and Mirin. Stir once and then place on a medium heat. Cook the rice according to the package directions. When rice is done cooking open lid and toss the chestnuts with the rice. Replace lid and set aside for 2 minutes, then serve, seasoned with gomashio.

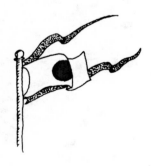

CHOU BELGIQUE

BELGIUM   SERVES: 6

*C*abbage and chestnuts are often served together in
central and northern Europe. There are several ways of
preparing this recipe but wine is nearly always in the list
of ingredients. This side dish is appropriate with beef,
pork or poultry as well as any wild game, but not recommended served with fish or seafood.

1 head red cabbage

1 Tablespoon butter or olive oil

1/4 cup (60 ml) red Bordeaux

6 whole cloves

1 bay leaf

salt and pepper

1/2 lb. (225 g) fresh chestnuts
or 1/4 lb. (110 g) dried, peeled
chestnuts

Chop the cabbage into thin
strips. Heat the oil in a
deep skillet and add all the
ingredients except the
chestnuts. Turn heat down
low, cover and simmer for
30 minutes. Meanwhile
roast and peel the chestnuts
(see page 25). If using
dried peeled nuts they must
already be rehydrated and
cooked (see page 27). Add
the chestnuts to the cabbage
and simmer for another 15
minutes. Remove bay leaf
and serve while still hot.

RED CABBAGE WITH CHESTNUTS

SWITZERLAND   SERVES: 6

*T*his *recipe is like the previous one, though a bit
sweeter with the addition of raisins and apples and a
more colorful dish to set upon the table. Try using half and
half of dark and golden raisins, or dried cranberries for an
even more festive look.*

**3/4 lb. (350 g) fresh chestnuts
or 1/2 lb. (225 g) dried peeled
chestnuts**

1 red cabbage

1/4 cup (60 ml) vinegar

1/2 cup (120 ml) boiling water

1 cup (250 ml) dry white wine

1/3 cup (70 g) dark raisins

1 teaspoon honey

**1 large or 2 small *Granny Smith*
apples**

**3 Tablespoons chestnut or
wheat flour**

Salt and pepper to taste

Peel the chestnuts by
lightly roasting, trying to
keep the nuts whole (see
page 25) or prepare dried
peeled chestnuts (see page
27). Set the nuts aside.
Chop the cabbage fine and
place in a metal bowl. Stir
in the vinegar and then the
boiling water; cover and set
aside for 10 minutes, then
drain thoroughly. Simmer
the cabbage in the wine with
the raisins and honey for 15
minutes. If more liquid is
needed add a little water.
Core and peel the apples
and chop into 3/4 inch (2
cm.) sized cubes. Add the
chopped apple and simmer
another few minutes.
Sprinkle flour over top and
stir in. Now add the
chestntus and lightly toss.
Simmer for another 15 or 20
minutes, gently stirring
from time to time until
moist but not soupy. Season
with salt and pepper and
serve.

BRUSSELS SPROUTS WITH CHESTNUTS

ENGLAND   SERVES: 6-8

A *very simple recipe and traditionally a part of the*
Christmas dinner of turkey or goose.

1 lb. (450 g) fresh chestnuts

**1 1/2 lbs. (700 g) small
Brussels sprouts**

2 Tablespoons (25 g) butter

salt and pepper

Roast and peel the chestnuts (see page 25), cover in a bowl and set aside. Wash and trim the Brussels sprouts, cut an X in the bottoms of their stems and place in a steamer and steam for about 10 minutes or until they are bright green and cooked through. Put the Brussels sprouts into the bowl of chestnuts. Add the butter and seasonings and toss gently until the butter is melted. Serve immediately or keep warm covered in the oven.

HARVEST TIMBALE

UNITED STATES   SERVES: 6

Timbale originally from Arabic "thabal", meaning drum, was a small round receptical for beverages. Later it became known as a larger bowl in which people shared their meal. In French cuisine the bowl was made of crust and filled with force meats, truffles and wonderful sauces. A Timbale can be made in a mold though, and still be called such. This recipe would do well in a pie crust with the vegetables and chestnut pieces mixed through. This dish is intended to be served at the American neighborhood feast, the potluck.

3 Tablespoons (40 g) butter

1 Tablespoon each of the following:
minced shallots
finely chopped celery
minced fresh thyme

1/2 Tablespoon fresh marjoram minced

dash cayenne

1/2 cup (120 ml) chicken broth

1/2 cup (120 g) chestnut purée

3 egg whites, beaten stiff

1 cup (130 g) each of the following:
fresh peas
fresh diced carrots
roasted chestnut pieces

Have the inside of a metal or ceramic ring mold greased and floured. Preheat oven at 350 F (180 C or gas 4). In a deep pan melt the butter and sauté the shallots, celery, herbs and spices. Add the chicken broth and the chestnut purée. Stir until smooth and well heated. Do not boil. Fold in the egg whites and pour into the ring mold. Place the ring mold in a large pan of very hot water in the oven. The ring mold should be just floating. Bake for 30-40 minutes or until a butter knife inserted comes out clean. Turn onto a warm serving plate and remove the mold. Have the peas and carrots lightly steamed and tossed together with the chestnut pieces. Fill the center of the ring with this mixture. Drizzle the sauce over the timbale and vegetables. Serve hot.

SAUCE FOR TIMBALE

2 Tablespoons (25 g) butter

1 1/2 cups (350 ml) chicken
broth

2 Tablespoons arrowroot
powder

1/2 cup (120 ml) water

1/4 teaspoon nutmeg

1/4 teaspoon ground white
pepper

1 egg yolk

1/2 cup (120ml) cream

2 Tablespoons lemon juice

1 Tablespoon fresh parsley

Melt the butter in a
saucepan over a medium
heat. Add the chicken
broth and bring to a boil.
Mix the arrowroot powder in
with the water and then stir
into the broth. Lower the
heat and stir until smooth.
Add spices. In a separate
bowl beat the egg yolk and
cream together, then slowly
add it to the sauce once the
heat is turned down to low.
Stir continually until thick.
Stir in the lemon juice and
chopped parsley and pour
over the Timbale.

KURI KINTON

JAPAN   SERVES: 6

*T*he Japanese New year (traditionally celebrated the first new moon after the sun enters Aquarius) is a time for absolving debts and renewing friendships. Chestnuts, although often served with a sweet adzuki bean paste, are mixed with yams in this recipe. This dish is served during the New Year and is meant to accompany smoked salmon.

1 lb. (450 g) fresh chestnuts

3/4 lb. (350 g) yams or sweet potatoes

2 Tablespoons light honey or sugar

2 Tablespoons Mirin (syrupy rice wine)

Pick out 10 of the largest chestnuts and slice their skin with a large 'X' , being certain not to cut into the meat. Cut the remaining chestnuts in half and boil all of the nuts for 10 minutes. With a slotted spoon pull out the whole chestnuts and peel them before they cool, trying to keep them intact. Set aside. Remove the rest of the nuts from the hot water and peel the same way. Peel and chop the yam into small pieces. Place in a heavy bottomed pot and put on a low heat. Add the honey or sugar. If it begins to stick add a very small amount of water. Add all but the whole chestnuts and simmer for 30 minutes or until it is all very tender. Pureé the cooked yams and chestnuts in a food mill, blender or masher. Return to pot and stir in the Mirin. Simmer for a few more minutes then let cool. Spoon onto a platter in a decorative shape and place the peeled whole chestnuts around.

STUFFED ACORN SQUASH

UNITED STATES   SERVES: 4-8

R ich in the essence of autumn with winter squash, black walnuts and maple syrup, this dish sets off a roast pig or wild turkey; or may be served simply as the main fare of a vegetarian meal with a wild greens salad and a creamy soup.

3/4 lb. (350 grams) fresh chestnuts

2 medium sized *Acorn* or *Delicata* squash

2 carrots

1/4 cup (50 g) Black walnuts or 1/2 cup (70 g) English walnuts

1/4 cup (50 g) raisins

dash salt

1/4 cup (50 g) butter

1/4 cup (85 ml) pure maple syrup

Preheat oven at 350 F (180 C or gas 4). Roast and peel the chestnuts (see page 25). Chop coarsely and set aside. Slice the squash in half lengthwise. Scoop out and discard the seeds. Chop the carrots and walnuts into small pieces. Mix the chestnuts, carrots, walnuts, raisins and salt, and fill the squash cavities heaping. Take bits of the butter and place over it all, cover and bake 45 minutes to one hour. Melt the remaining butter with the maple syrup and drizzle sparingly over the top before serving.

57

POLISH NUT CROQUETTES

POLAND   SERVES: 6

Chestnut croquettes can be sweet and served as a pastry or, as in this case, can be quite savory and almost meaty. Serve with ham and a robust wine.

1/2 lb. (225 g) fresh chestnuts

1 1/2 cups (350 g) dry mashed potatoes

1/4 cup (50 g) walnuts chopped

3 eggs

2 Tablespoons fresh parsley

salt and pepper

1 cup (80 g) fine bread crumbs

1/4 cup (55 ml) cooking oil

1 large onion

1/2 lb. (225 g) mushrooms

2 Tablespoons (25 g) butter

2 Tablespoons flour

2 lbs. (900 g) fresh sauerkraut

Cut chestnuts in half and boil until tender. Peel while still hot. Mash the chestnuts and mix with the potatoes, walnuts, eggs, minced parsley, salt and pepper into a thick paste. Form patties with a spoon and your fingers. Roll in the breadcrumbs, and pan fry in hot cooking oil, turning so both sides become golden crispy brown. When done, set on paper to drain. In a separate pan chop the onion and mushrooms and sauté in the butter. Add the flour and stir till browned. Add the sauerkraut; stir and simmer for 10 minutes. Spread the sauerkraut mixture out on a warmed serving plate. Arrange the croquettes on top and serve.

LEEKS AND CHESTNUTS

UNITED STATES   SERVES: 6

uring the winter months nearly every other meal at our home contains fresh garden leeks, and we never tire of them. A few shakes of raspberry vinegar gives this dish a pleasant fruity 'tang' which sends you back to warm summer days. Serve with meat loaf or chicken.

1 lb. (450 g) fresh chestnuts or
1/2 lb. (225 g) dried peeled
chestnuts

3 cups (750 ml) chicken broth

3 large mild leeks

2 Tablespoons olive oil

raspberry vinegar

Roast and peel the fresh chestnuts (see page 25), or soak dried peeled chestnuts overnight and drain. Put the chestnuts in a medium sized pot and add the chicken broth. Put on a medium heat and simmer covered until liquid is nearly gone. Meanwhile clean leeks and chop off the scraggly roots and the tops, leaving about an inch (3 cm.) of green. Slice lengthwise and rinse any remaining grit. Chop into 3/4 inch (2 cm) sections. Sauté the leeks in the olive oil until tender. Add the chestnuts and what is left of the broth. Stir well and keep warm until served. Sprinkle a little bit of raspberry vinegar over all before serving.

CHESTNUT SALAD

UNITED STATES   SERVES: 4

*S*imilar variations of this recipe appear often in American cooking magazines dating as far back as 1896. It is important to use only fresh chestnuts for the best flavor.

1 lb. (450 g) fresh chestnuts

3 large stalks diced celery

1 large apple

1 Tablespoon mayonaise or plain yogurt

2 teaspoons raspberry vinegar

1 head *Romaine* lettuce

Roast and peel the chestnuts (see page 25). Chill and then slice and put in a bowl with the diced celery. Peel, core and chop the apple and add to the bowl. Stir in the mayonaise or yogurt and vinegar and spoon onto a bed of lettuce.

Chapter Five

MAIN FARE

CORNISH HENS WITH CHESTNUTS

ENGLAND   SERVES: 4

The Duke of Argyll, during the 18th century, was often served a more complicated version of this dish by his cook, Charles Carter. No doubt his combination of oysters and chestnuts to "fill the bellies" of the Cornish hens is what has inspired many cooks since then to use those same ingredients to stuff the holiday bird. The original recipe requires the bird to be put in a bladder, tied shut, and then boiled. I've found that the pressure cooker does a more than adequate job.

1 lb. (450 g) fresh
    chestnuts or 1/2 lb. (225 g)
    dried peeled chestnuts
2 Cornish hens 1 1/4 lbs. (560g)
    each
3 cups (750 ml) water
1 stalk celery
salt and pepper
1/2 cup (150 g) shelled oysters
1 egg
1/4 teaspoon nutmeg
arrowroot powder
1/4 cup (60 g) sugar
3 Tablespoons frozen orange
    juice concentrate

Roast and peel the fresh chestnuts (see page 25), or prepare the dried chestnuts (see page 27). Drain and set aside. Wash and pat dry the birds. Clean the giblets and put in a pot with the water and celery and set it to boil with a lid. Rub the birds with salt and pepper inside and out. Chop up the chestnuts and the oysters and mix together with the egg and nutmeg. Season with salt and pepper. This mixture may be a bit runny but that's alright. Spoon half of it into each birds cavity. You may have to sew the neck shut first. Then, once filled, sew the cavity shut, tucking in the tails. Place the birds on a rack in a pressure cooker. Add 3/4 cup (175 ml) water and seal the lid. Place on a high heat and cook for 12 minutes once the cooker has reached 15 lbs. pressure. Then allow to cool slowly. Strain 2 cups of the stock (from the back burner) and heat in a saucepan. Season the stock with salt and pepper. In a separate cup mix the sugar and arrowroot powder in with the orange juice concentrate. Pour this slowly into the boiling stock while stirring. Stir this until thick. Place the hens on a platter decorated with greens. Pour sauce over all and serve.

PORK AND CHESTNUTS

PORTUGAL   SERVES: 6

This dish is perfectly suited to prepare on the campfire in a dutch oven. Serve with a thick crusted bread and a salad.

2 lbs. (900 g) fresh chestnuts or 1 1/4 lb. (560 g) dried peeled chestnuts

4 Tablespoons (55 ml) olive oil

2 cloves garlic

2 large onions

4 carrots

1 stalk celery

6 large pork chops

1 cup (250 ml) white wine

2 Tablespoons tomato paste

1 bay leaf

1 Tablespoon fresh thyme

2 teaspoons fresh parsley

salt and pepper to taste

Roast and peel the fresh chestnuts and set aside (see page 25) or soak dried peeled chestnuts overnight. Heat the oil in a large heavy pot (a deep iron skillet with a lid works best). Chop the garlic, onion, carrots and celery and add to the oil. Trim the fat from the meat, pat dry and add to the pot. Brown on both sides. Add wine, tomato paste and bay. Finely chop the herbs and add to the pot. If using dried peeled chestnuts add those now and then enough water to cover it all. Put on the lid and once it begins to simmer turn down the heat and let it cook for 2 hours. If using fresh, frozen or canned chestnuts add them after the first 2 hours and let simmer another 40 minutes, only adding water if the pot is too dry.

ROAST LAMB WITH CHESTNUTS

GREECE   SERVES: 6-8

No need for lots of complicated flavors and sauces to enjoy a rich and toothsome meal. The Greek do have a way of bringing out the best in foods with the simplest of seasonings. This dish is no exception. Serve with rice.

salt and pepper

1 leg of lamb

juice of 1 lemon

6 sprigs fresh rosemary

2 lbs. (900 g) chestnuts

Preheat oven at 350F (180C or gas 4). Wash the lamb and rub with salt and pepper. Sprinkle with lemon juice and insert small sprigs of rosemary into the flesh with the help of a small sharp knife. Roast in the oven in a deep roasting pan allowing 30 minutes for every pound of meat. Baste often with the drippings and turn the meat so it roasts evenly. Roast and peel the chestnuts (see page 25) and add to the lamb after the first hour of baking.

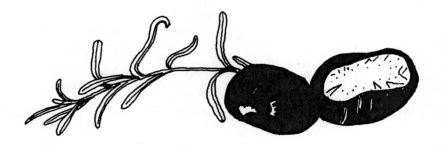

LAMBCHOP AND CHESTNUT RAGOÛT

FRANCE   SERVES: 4

*R*agoût, *from the French verb ragoûter, which means to bring back ones appetite, has been enjoyed since ancient times. A ragoût is simply a meat and vegetable stew. This one is baked in the oven in a deep casserole with a lid.*

1 lb. (450 g) fresh chestnuts or 1/2 lb. (225 g) dried peeled chestnuts

8 lamb chops

2 Tablespoons olive oil

salt and pepper

1 teaspoon thyme

2 cloves garlic crushed

2 onions

1 teaspoon parsley

1 cup (250 ml) beef broth

1 cup (250 ml) sherry

Roast and peel the chestnuts (see page 25), or prepare dried chestnuts (see page 27). Set aside. Preheat oven to 350F (180C or gas 4). Cut off as much of the fat as possible from the meat and place four of the lamb chops in the bottom of a casserole dish in which the oil has been spread. Sprinkle a bit of salt and pepper over it. Add half the thyme and half of the garlic. Slice the onions into thin wedges and place half of them on top. Then add half of the chestnuts. Make another layer like the first and finish with a dash of olive oil and parsley. Heat the broth and add the wine and pour this over the casserole. Cover and bake for one hour.

CHESTNUT VEGETABLE STEW

SOUTHERN FRANCE   SERVES: 6

1 lb. (450 g) fresh chestnuts
1 onion
2 Tablespoons (25 g) butter
2 large cabbage leaves
2 carrots
1 turnip
2 potatoes
2 stalks celery with green tops
3 cups (750 ml) chicken broth
1 Tablespoon fresh parsley
chopped

Roast and peel the chestnuts (see page 25). Chop the onion and sauté in the butter in the bottom of a soup pot. Chop the vegetables and add to the onion. Add the chestnuts and the chicken stock. Set to simmer and let cook for 30 minutes. Add the parsley before serving. Season with salt and pepper to taste.

CHESTNUTS AND PORK

ENGLAND   SERVES: 6

1 1/2 lbs. (700 g) fresh
chestnuts or 1 lb. (450 g) dried
peeled chestnuts

2 lbs. (900 g) pork loin

2 Tablespoons olive oil

1 sprig rubbed sage

2 cloves garlic crushed

1 cup (250 ml) red wine

1 1/2 cups (350 ml) hot broth

salt and pepper

Preheat the oven at 300F (150C or gas 2). Roast and peel the fresh chestnuts or prepare the dried chestnuts (see pages 25 or 27). Remove bone, fat and gristle from the pork. Chop meat into 1 inch (3 cm) sized chunks. Heat the oil in a casserole dish and brown the meat. Add the sage and garlic. Add the wine and the heated broth. Cover and place in the oven for 2 hours. Season with salt and pepper to taste. Serve with rice.

MAR HI GAI

CHINA   SERVES: 2

1/2 lb. (225 g) fresh chestnuts
or 1/4 lb. (110 grams) dried
peeled chestnuts

Breast of one chicken

1 Tablespoon peanut oil

1 clove garlic crushed

4 thick slices fresh ginger

2 teaspoons sherry

1/2 teaspoon honey

ground pepper

1/2 cup (120 ml) hot water

soy sauce

Roast and peel the chestnuts
(see page 25), or prepare
the dried peeled chestnuts
(see page 27). Set aside.
Remove any skin, bone or fat
from the meat and chop into
pieces. Heat the oil in a
wok or skillet. Throw in the
garlic, stir. Add ginger,
stir. Add chicken, brown
all sides. Stir in sherry,
honey, pepper, hot water
and a shake or two of soy
sauce. Cover and simmer 30
minutes. Coarsely chop the
chestnuts and add to the
chicken. Remove lid and
simmer until liquid
reduces. Remove ginger and
season with soy sauce to
taste. Serve with rice.

RED DUCK WITH PEAR AND CHESTNUT

CHINA   SERVES: 6

*P*robably the most well known of Chinese recipes is
Peking Duck, but there are many other wonderful ways
to prepare duck. This recipe calls for Asian pears, which
are crisp pears that have an aromatic flavor, hinting of fruit
blossoms. A good friend and accomplished horticulturalist,
Buddy Beck, grows these pears in Western Oregon and
recommends the variety Kosui as most suited for a stir fry.

**1/2 lb. (225 g) fresh chestnuts
or 1/4 lb. (110 g) dried peeled
chestnuts**

5 lb. (2.25 kg) duck

3 green onions

3 thick slices of ginger root

1/4 cup (60 ml) soy sauce

**2 Tablespoons Yellow bean
paste (miso)**

1/4 cup (60 ml) sherry

1 teaspoon arrowroot powder

1 *Kosui* Asian Pear

2 teaspoons sugar

Roast and peel fresh
chestnuts or prepare the
dried peeled chestnuts (see
pages 25 or 27). Wash and
dry the duck. Cut it into 3
inch (8 cm.) pieces and
place in bottom of a large
pot. Cover with water and
bring to a boil. Boil for 10
minutes, then turn heat
down to a gentle simmer.
Chop the green onions into
large pieces and add to the
pot. Add the ginger, soy
sauce, miso and chestnuts.
Simmer for 45 minutes.
Add the sherry and simmer
for another 40 minutes.
Remove the ginger root.
Drain most of the juices
from the duck into a smaller
pan and heat. Add the
arrowroot powder (mixed in
a small amount of water) to
the juices in the small pan
and simmer until thickened.
Peel, core and cut the pear
into wedges. Dredge in the
sugar and add to the sauce.
Simmer about 5 minutes or
until pear is tender.
Arrange the duck on a warm
platter with the chestnuts
and pear slices all around.
Pour the sauce over it all.
Serve with rice.

TENDERLOIN FRUIT MINGLE

UNITED STATES   SERVES: 2-4

*T*his recipe calls for dried sweet black cherries which are not readily available but are worth the trouble to seek out. If you have a food dryer, I recommend putting up a store for yourself.

1 lb. (450 g) fresh chestnuts

4 *Granny Smith* apples

15 dried black cherries

1 teaspoon sugar

1 cup (250 ml) Burgundy

4 venison or small beef tenderloins 1 inch (3 cm) thick

2 Tablespoons olive oil

salt and pepper

several mint sprigs

Roast and peel the chestnuts (see page 25). Peel, core and slice the apples into thin wedges. Slice the cherries in half. Place the chestnuts, apples and cherries in a glass bowl. Sprinkle with sugar and pour the wine over them. Cover and set aside for 30 minutes. Cut the steaks into 1 inch (3 cm.) sized chunks. In a heavy skillet, heat the oil, brown the meat and cook until done. Set the meat aside, keeping it warm. Take the fruit and chestnuts and add them to the meat juices in the pan and the wine. Simmer for 20 minutes. Add the meat and heat through. Season with salt and pepper and serve on a bed of fresh mint.

HIND ROAST WITH CHESTNUT AND MUSHROOM SAUCE

EUROPE   SERVES: 6

B oletus edulis, also known as Cep, Porcino, or Penny Bun, is the most sought for wild mushroom in the Western world. Unless you gather your own, 450 grams of Boletus may be a bit of a strain on the pocketbook, but use at least as many as you can afford. This lusciously savory roast will melt in your mouth. Serve with parsnip and potato pureé and steamed green vegetables.

1 venison roast boned
1 onion
2 cloves garlic
1 bay leaf
1 bottle hearty red wine
5 slices fresh bacon
1 lb. (450 g) fresh chestnuts
1-2 cups (250 - 475 ml) stock
1 lb. (450 g) *Boletus edulis*
    mushrooms
3 Tablespoons olive oil
3 Tablespoons arrowroot
    powder
1 cup (225 ml) sour cream

Wash the meat well and place in a container which is not metal or plastic. Slice the onion thin and crush the garlic. Add these and the bay to the roast. Pour the wine over it all. The meat should be covered in wine. Cover and let sit in the refrigerator for 12 hours. The meat will look purple. Wrap bacon around the roast and secure with toothpicks. Place the roast in a heavy pan and bake in the oven at 450F (230C or gas 8) for the first 20 minutes. Then reduce the heat to 350F (180C or gas 4) and bake for 20 minutes for each pound (450 grams) of meat. Watch the meat towards the end to be sure not to overcook it. Use of a meat thermometer is recommended. Meanwhile roast and peel the chestnuts (see page 25) and boil, just covered in stock. Slice and sauté the mushrooms in the olive oil, when cooked through add to the chestnuts. Stir the arrowroot powder into 1 cup (250 ml.) of the marinade. Add to the chestnuts and mushrooms in the stock and stir until thick. Fold in the sour cream and keep warm, but do not boil. Serve this roast in a deep sided serving dish with the sauce poured over it.

CHESTNUT STIR FRY

CHINA   SERVES: 4

*T*his is a light, quick and easy vegetarian dish.

1/2 lb. (225 g) fresh chestnuts

7 oz. package (200 grams) of
bean thread noodles

1/4 lb. (110 g) *Shiitake*
mushrooms

1 medium zucchini squash

3 Tablespoons (45 ml) peanut
oil

4 thin slices ginger

1 clove garlic crushed

1 small can bamboo shoots

soy sauce

Roast and peel chesnuts and
set aside (see page 25).
Place bean threads in a pan
and cover with boiling
water, place lid on and set
aside. Slice the mushrooms
long and thin and set aside.
Slice the zucchini into 2
inch (5 cm.) spears and set
aside. Heat the oil in a wok,
(or fry pan), and add the
ginger and garlic to the hot
oil. Stir for 1 minute, then
add the mushrooms and
bamboo shoots. Stir for 2
minutes, then add the
zucchini and chestnuts and
stir for another 4 minutes.
Remove ginger. Drain and
chop bean threads, add to
the stir fry and cook
another 2 minutes. Season
with soy sauce and serve.

MUSHROOMS AND CHESTNUTS

EARLY AMERICA   SERVES: 4

*S*ome *of the most resourceful, productive, peaceful and
honest pioneers during the formation of the New World
were the Shaking Quakers, more commonly known as the
Shakers. These people, numbering thousands during the
late 1700's, contributed to much of what is called Ameri-
cana. Simplicity and quality marked everything they did in
thought,as well as in deed. In the kitchen this meant
utilizing food closest to its natural state and at its freshest.
The Sisters understood the value of chestnuts, which they
gleaned from the forests of the Northeast and used exten-
sively, especially in vegetarian dishes. This dish was often
served with baked potatoes.*

2 lbs. (900 g) fresh chestnuts	Roast and peel the chestnuts (see page 25) and chop them
1 1/2 lbs. (700 g) mushrooms	coarsely. Set these aside. Clean and quarter the
2 Tablespoons (25 g) butter	mushrooms. Heat a large skillet and sauté the
2 Tablespoons flour	quartered mushrooms in the butter until slightly
2 cups (475 ml) light cream	browned. Stir in the flour and brown. Then slowly add
salt and pepper	the cream, salt, pepper and chopped parsley. Add the
1 Tablespoon fresh parsley	chestnuts and heat through.

Boletus edulis

73

RICE AND CHESTNUT PATTIES

EARLY AMERICA   SERVES: 4

This is another meatless Shaker dish and represents a complete source of protein.

1/2 lb. (225 g) fresh chestnuts

1/2 cup (40 g) crushed dried bread crumbs

2 cups (400 g) cooked rice

2 eggs

1 teaspoon chopped fresh parsley

2 Tablespoons light cream

1 beaten egg

1/4 cup (35 g) flour

1/4 cup (60 ml) cooking oil

Roast and peel the chestnuts (see page 25) and chop coarsely. Mix all but the beaten egg, flour and cooking oil together and form into patties. Dip the patties into the beaten egg and roll in the flour. Heat the oil in a skillet and fry the patties, turning to brown both sides.

TRUFFLES AND CHESTNUTS

UNITED STATES   SERVES: 8

Ahh . . . truffles . . . there are no words in the human language to describe the experience of truffles. This recipe calls for the Oregon White Truffle, but any edible species will do just as well. This dish makes for a nice appetizer before a grand meal, or simply served with onion and cabbage soup on a blustery evening, with crusty French bread and port wine.

several *Oregon White* truffle mushrooms

1/4 cup (60 ml.) brandy

1 lb. (450 g) fresh chestnuts

3 medium Yellow Finn potatoes

1 lb. (450 g) bacon strips

With a soft dry brush, lightly scrub any dirt from the truffles and soak them in a good brandy or cognac for about an hour. Lightly roast and peel the chestnuts (see page 25). Cut the potatoes into 1 inch (2cm.) cubes. Steam the chestnuts and potatoes for 5 minutes. Arrange the potatoes, chestnuts and truffles on an oven proof glass casserole dish. Lay strips of bacon over it all and broil until the bacon is crispy.

STUFFINGS

*L*ong ago, I imagine that the ever resourceful cook found the cavity of the gutted bird the perfect container for braising a few morsels of viands and vegetables. We soon discovered how satisfying this mutual transfusion of flavors could be and have ever after, grown quite partial to this glorious mélange, simply, but aptly named, "stuffing". The stuffing recipe is the most personal of all. It's the cook's signature on a masterpiece of a feast. There is nothing quite as heart warming and reasuring as the holiday stuffing and everyone's mother most assuredly makes the best.

Simple or complex in flavors, the stuffing uses the best of what is available and so there can be found regional commonality in ingredients. The list of ingredients is nearly limitless, but here are a few: Starches, such as chestnut, rice, wild rice, cornbread, any bread, crackers, potatoes and grain meals. These absorb juices and flavors. Fruits, including: apples, figs, prunes, raisins, currants and oranges. These add sweetness and tartness. Nuts such as chestnuts, walnuts, pine nuts, peanuts, pecans, pistachios, macadamias and sunflower seeds, all of which provide flavor and mostly texture. All sorts of viands such as: oysters, sausages, bacon, hard cooked eggs, giblets and sweetbreads. The vegetables: carrot, turnip, celery, sweet potato, eggplant and peppers, be it sweet bells or hot chilies. Mushrooms from button to truffle. Then there are the seasonings. Typically sage, marjoram, thyme, salt and pepper, but cinnamon, cayenne and nutmeg can find a place in the composition as well.

In America the most common way to serve chestnuts is in the holiday turkey stuffing. Think of them as a flavorful and sweet starch which will absorb the other flavors while still imparting some of their own. They can provide an interesting texture when used whole or in pieces or act as a back drop for other textures when used as a puréeOn the following pages are 10 stuffing recipes representing six cultures. Each one different than the next and all traditional and delicious, but then . . . I've never tasted a bad stuffing!

TURKEY ROASTING INSTRUCTIONS

The basic procedure for roasting a turkey is as follows: Preheat the oven to 450F (230C or gas 8). Begin with the turkey at room temperature and wash it with warm water. Pat dry. Place the turkey on a rack uncovered, in a roasting pan, breast side up. Stuff the cavities loosely with stuffing and skewer or sew shut. Place in the oven and reduce the heat to 350F (180C or gas 4). If using a meat thermometer, it should be inserted between the thigh and the body, taking care not to let the tip of the probe touch the bone. Cook the bird until an internal temperature of 190F (88C) is reached. Allow 25 minutes of cooking time per pound (450 grams) for birds up to six pounds (2.75 grams) and 20 minutes per pound (450 grams) for larger birds. Baste frequently. To tell if the turkey is done without an internal thermometer, prick the skin on the inside of the thigh and when the juices run clear, the bird is done. Any stuffing that won't fit in the bird can be wrapped in foil or placed in a greased casserole dish with a lid and baked in the oven along side the turkey for the last 45 minutes.

CHESTNUT STUFFING FROM GREECE

GREECE   SERVES: 6

1 lb. (450 g) fresh chestnuts

1/2 cup (110 g) butter

1 diced onion

3/4 cup (175 ml) milk

3 sprigs fresh sage

1 bay leaf

1/2 teaspoon thyme

1/2 cup (40 g) bread crumbs

salt and pepper

7 lb. (3 kg) turkey

juice of one lemon

1/2 cup (120 ml) hot water

Roast and peel the chestnuts (see page 25). Crumble and set aside. Melt 3 Tablespoons (40 grams) of the butter in a sauce pan and sauté diced onion until soft. Add the milk and the herbs and simmer for 2 minutes. Place the chestnuts and bread crumbs in a large bowl, pour the butter and milk mixture over the bread and chestnuts, mix well until milk is absorbed. Season with salt and pepper. Next, rub cleaned turkey with salt. Add the stuffing and skewer shut. Place the turkey in a large pan suitable for roasting. Melt the remaining butter and add lemon juice. Use this to baste the turkey. Add the hot water to the baking pan and bake in a preheated oven, basting periodically (see page 77).

JEWISH CHESTNUT STUFFING

JEWISH   SERVES: 8

1 1/2 lb. (700 kg) fresh chestnuts

4 cups (1 liter) stock

turkey giblets from the turkey

2 Tablespoons (25 g) butter

3/4 cup (60 g) fresh bread crumbs

2 Tablespoons fresh parsley chopped

salt and pepper

2 beaten eggs

8 lb. (3.5 kg) turkey

Peel the chestnuts by boiling, (see page 26). Cook the peeled chestnuts in enough stock to cover, until very tender. Put them through a ricer or a food processor and set aside. Chop the giblets fine and in a small skillet sauté them in the butter, then mix together with the bread crumbs, parsley, salt and pepper, and chestnut purée. Add the beaten egg and mix thoroughly. Stuff and skewer the turkey. Place in a covered roasting pan and bake in a preheated oven (See page 77).

DINDE ALA FRANCAISE

FRANCE   SERVES: 6-8

1 lb. (450 g) fresh chestnuts

8 lb. (3.5 kg) turkey

olive oil

salt and pepper

1 1/2 lb. (700 g) chopped pork

3 medium sized truffles

1/2 cup (120 ml) hot water

SAUCE:

2 shallots minced

1/2 cup (110 g) butter

1/2 cup (70 grams) flour

4 cups (1 liter) stock

1/2 cup (120 ml) white wine

1/2 Tablespoon fresh parsley

Roast and peel the chestnuts (see page 25). Chop and set aside. Rub the clean turkey with olive oil, salt and pepper. Brown the pork in a skillet and add to the chestnuts. Thinly slice the truffles and mix in with the pork and chestnuts. Stuff the turkey loosely and skewer shut. Place in a roasting pan, add the hot water and cover. Bake in preheated oven, (see page 77). Baste often. Serve with white wine sauce.

For the sauce, sauté the shallots in the butter in a sauce pan. Stir in the flour and sauté until shallots are tender and the flour is lightly browned. Slowly stir in the stock and let simmer about 10 minutes or until well thickened. Add the wine and simmer another few minutes. Add chopped parsley and bring to the table in a sauce boat.

RUSSIAN CHESTNUT STUFFING

FORMER SOVIET UNION   SERVES: 6-8

2 lbs. (900 g) fresh chestnuts

3 cups (750 ml) milk

2 Tablespoons (25 g) butter

6 slices stale bread

3 Tablespoons currants

1 teaspoon ground cinnamon

salt and pepper

8 lb. (3.5 kg) turkey

1/2 cup (120 ml) hot water

1/4 cup (60 ml) port wine

1 teaspoon lemon juice

6 carrots

4 celery stalks

1/2 lb. (225 g) ham

8 peppercorns

1 large bay leaf

Boil and peel the chestnuts (see page 26). In a sauce pan add enough milk to cover the chestnuts and gently simmer until tender. Add butter and mash with a potato masher or put through a ricer. In a large bowl crumble the bread, then add the mashed chestnuts and let stand 15 minutes. Add more milk if the bread and chestnuts are too dry. Mix currants, cinnamon, salt and pepper in with the bread and chestnuts. Stuff and skewer a clean turkey. Place in a deep roasting pan and add hot water. Mix the wine and lemon juice to baste the turkey. Bake in preheated oven (see page 77). Chop the vegetables and the ham. Place the vegetables, ham, peppercorns and bay in the roasting pan around the turkey to bake for the last one and a half hours. Baste often with the juices in the pan.

BRAZILIAN STUFFING

BRAZIL   SERVES: 6

C hestnuts in Brazil are harvested from trees first planted by the Spanish colonists long ago. This recipe blends Old World chestnuts with New World cassava, or manioc, which has been a main staple of the South American natives even before Columbus first set foot on that beautiful wild land. Sweet manioc can be served as a vegetable or dried and ground into a flour. It is different than the bitter manioc rendered to make tapioca. Sweet manioc flour may be difficult to find, but corn meal makes a fine substitute.

1 1/4 lbs. (560 g) fresh chestnuts

2 1/2 cups (600 ml) beef stock

1 small onion

2 Tablespoons (25 g) butter

1 cup (160 g) sweet manioc flour or corn meal

1/4 lb. (110 g) pitted prunes

1/4 lb. (110 g) golden raisins

1/4 teaspoon thyme

1/4 teaspoon marjoram

salt and pepper

8 lb. (3.5 kg) turkey

Roast and peel the chestnuts (see page 25) and simmer in 1 1/2 cups (350 ml) of the beef stock until chestnuts are tender. Chop the onion into small pieces and sauté in the butter until translucent. Add the flour or meal and stir well, until toasted. Chop the prunes and add them with the raisins to the onion and flour. Mix in the seasonings and add enough broth to moisten, about 1 cup (250 ml). Loosely stuff the bird, cover and bake (see page 77).

COLONIAL CHESTNUT STUFFING

COLONIAL AMERICA   SERVES: 6-8

*R*oasted chestnuts were added to the gravy when the
turkey held this stuffing. If you are not using the
small nuts of the American chestnut for such a gravy, then
chop larger chestnuts into quarter sections.

2 lbs. (900 g) fresh chestnuts	Roast and peel the chestnuts (see page 25). Melt butter
4 Tablespoons (50 g) butter	and add to the nuts in a bowl. Mash with a potato
salt and pepper	masher and blend well with salt and pepper. Stuff the
8 lb. (3.5 kg) turkey	turkey and bake in a covered roasting pan (see page 77).

DEEP SOUTHERN STUFFING

SOUTHEASTERN UNITED STATES   SERVES: 6

1/2 lb. (225 g) fresh chestnuts	Roast and peel the chestnuts (see page 25). Crumble and
1/2 lb. (225 g) dried figs	set aside. Remove the stems
boiling water	from the figs and put the
1 onion	figs in a glass or metal
1/2 of a bell pepper	bowl. Pour enough boiling
1/4 cups (50 g) butter	water to cover them and let
1/2 cup (120 g) canned *Mandarin* orange sections, drained	sit for 10 minutes. Chop the onion and bell pepper and sauté in the butter
2 Tablespoons fresh parsley chopped	until onions are translucent. Drain the figs
1/2 teaspoon thyme	and place in a large mixing
1/8 teaspoon red pepper	bowl. Add all other
salt and pepper to taste	ingredients but the broth
2 cups (160 g) bread crumbs	and mix well. Add enough
1 cup (250 ml) chicken broth	broth to moisten, then stuff
8 lb. (3.5 kg) turkey	the turkey and bake (see page 77).

CHESTNUT AND CORNBREAD STUFFING

UNITED STATES   SERVES: 6-8

T he first settlers in the Appalachian region cleared old growth forests to plant corn and other crops. It was a hard way to live and meals were utilitarian in simplicity. Though this recipe reflects the hard and simple times, its flavor and texture are worthy of a great meal.

1 lb. (450 g) fresh chestnuts or
1/2 lb. (225 g) dried, peeled
chestnuts

1 onion minced

1/4 cup (50 g) butter

3 cups (300 g) cornbread
crumbled

1/4 teaspoon each of the
following:
rubbed sage
thyme
marjoram

1 Tablespoon fresh parsley
chopped

salt and pepper

hot water

8 lb. (3.5 kg) turkey

Roast and peel the fresh chestnuts or prepare the dried, peeled chestnuts, (see pages 25 or 27), and chop. Sauté the onion in the butter until soft. In a large metal bowl mix well all the ingredients, except the water. Slowly mix in enough hot water to moisten it well. Stuff and bake the turkey in a preheated oven (see page 77).

BLUEGRASS STUFFING

UNITED STATES   SERVES: 6-8

1/2 lb. (225 g) fresh chestnuts

1 cup (225 g) hot mashed
sweet potato

2 Tablespoons (25 g) butter

1/2 cup (120 ml) cream

salt and pepper

8 lb. (3.5 kg) turkey

Roast and peel the chestnuts
(see page 25) and mash with
a potato masher. Mix with
the mashed sweet potato.
Stir in butter, cream, salt
and pepper. Stuff the
turkey, skewer shut and
bake in a preheated oven
(see page 77).

ROAST GOOSE WITH CHESTNUTS AND APPLES

GREECE   SERVES: 8

*W*hen roasting a goose one must prepare it by pricking the skin, (not the meat), with a fork all over. This helps release the oils in the skin. The surface needs to be heated by pre-roasting (before stuffing), in a preheated oven at 400F (200C or gas 6) for 15 minutes; or place the goose in a pan sitting up tall with the head up and drizzle about 1/4 cup (55 ml) very hot oil over it to make the skin sizzle, being certain to cover the whole bird. After the goose is stuffed, place it on a rack in a good sized roasting pan and cover. An internal thermometer is quite handy. As with turkey, roast 20 minutes for each pound (450 g) of bird. Uncover the last 1/2 hour and baste frequently to attain a golden skin.

3/4 lb. (350 g) fresh chestnuts

8 lb. (3.5 kg) goose

1 teaspoon salt

1 lemon cut in half

1 large onion

1/4 cup (50 grams) butter

4 *Granny Smith* apples

1/2 cup (70 g) pine nuts

6 sprigs fresh parsley chopped

1 teaspoon cinnamon

1/4 cup (60ml) milk

Roast and peel the chestnuts (see page 25). Chop coarsely and set aside. Wash and dry the goose and remove any excess fat. Prepare as mentioned above. Rub the skin with the salt and the half of a lemon. Chop the onion and sauté in the butter until soft. Peel, core and chop the apples and add to the onion. Continue heating. Stir in the pine nuts, chestnuts, parsley, cinnamon and milk. Simmer for a few minutes then stuff the goose loosely and tie shut. Roast as explained above.

Chapter Six

BREADS
and
PASTA

BASIC CHESTNUT PASTA

ITALY   SERVES: 4

*T*his pasta is incredibly delicious and is best served
with a very light sauce. An arugula pesto, clear broth, or
just butter, all go well with this noodle.

1 cup (140 g) pastry flour

1/2 cup (80 g) chestnut flour

2 large eggs

Mix flours together well and form a mound with an open center. Add eggs to the hole in the center and beat with a fork. Gradually mix flour and eggs together to form a smooth, tender, but not sticky ball. Add more pastry flour if necessary.

Knead the dough on a floured surface for about 5 minutes. Cover with a sightly damp cloth and let set for 20 minutes. Work with half of the dough at a time, rolling it out on a floured surface until about 1/16 inch (1.5 mm) thick sheet. Lightly dust with flour and roll up the sheet. Cut into slender sections and then unroll to reveal long flat noodles. Hang to dry for about 2 hours. Cook in boiling salted water for 3-5 minutes.

*A*nother way to shape the pasta dough is in a form called Gnocchi which is literally translated as "knuckles". This is a thick round noodle, concave on one side and with many ridges on the other. A wonderful form for holding a thin sauce. To create gnocchi, roll the dough into a long cylinder about the thickness of your ring finger. Then slice into knuckle length sections. With a flour dusted index finger on one side and a flour dusted fork on the other, press and roll the cylinder, thus forming a bowl with your finger and ridges with the fork. These are thicker than flat noodles and should be boiled a bit longer, and are often served like dumplings in a broth.

GNOCCHI

ITALY   SERVES: 4

*T*his *pasta, also called gnocchi, is more like a dumpling which is made with potato or, in this case, chestnut purée. Served in bowls with the broth or use the broth to make a thick gravy and pour over gnocchi.*

1 lb. (450 g) fresh chestnuts

1 large egg

salt and pepper

pastry flour

4 cups (1 liter) chicken or beef broth

Roast and peel the chestnuts (see page 25) and chop fine in a food processor. The idea is to have a smooth texture as in a purée, but as dry as possible. Mix in the egg, salt and pepper and add just enough flour to keep the dough from being sticky. Roll out dough on floured surface into slender, (finger width), ropes. Cut up into knuckle length sections. Place into simmering broth with a slotted spoon and gently cook until centers are done.

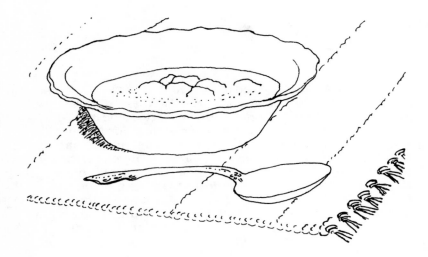

CASTAGNACCIO

ITALY   SERVES: 6

*T*he suffix 'accio' meaning rough, refers to the unrefined
aspects of this cake. Supposedly originating from the
mountains of Tuscany, it was made in any village that had
chestnuts and where the people were impoverished due to
war. Tradition prevails and castagnaccio is still prepared
today, perhaps in gratitude to the chestnut, or maybe
simply because it tastes so good.

2 cups (350 g) chestnut flour

6 Tablespoons (80 ml) olive oil

salt

1 cup (250 ml) water

1 small handful pine nuts

1 small handfull golden raisins

1 sprig fresh rosemary

Preheat oven to 325 F (170
C or gas 3). Put the flour in
a bowl with 2 Tablespoons
of the oil and a pinch of
salt. Stir and slowly add
the water, mixing all the
while to eliminate any
lumps. Add enough water to
form a very thick batter or a
thin dough. Pour into a 8
inch (20 cm) cake pan in
which the remaining oil has
been spread. Smooth down.
The olive oil should creep
up the sides and spill over
the top of the cake. Firmly
press the pine nuts and
raisins into the surface and
press the rosemary in the
middle of the top. Place in
a preheated oven and bake
for about 35 minutes.

SIGNORA BENZO'S CASTAGNACCIO

ITALY   SERVES: 6

*C*astagnaccio, being a traditional Italian mountain food is
all well and good, but since times aren't so lean for
these hearty hillfolk, the foods they serve aren't so sparce.
The welcome addition of wheat, milk and eggs hasn't changed
the name, but certainly makes a more agreeable bread. This
recipe was given to me by Signora Benzo. The Benzos live in
Perlo, a small village on the northern slopes of the Maritime
Alps, where they harvest large quantities of chestnuts every
year for drying.

Use the same ingredients and directions as the previous
recipe, but for the following exceptions: Replace 3/4 cup
(120 g) of the chestnut flour with a equal amount of pastry
flour. Replace the water with milk. Add 2 beaten eggs and
1/2 teaspoon vanilla extract. Proceed as in the previous
castagnaccio recipe.

FRITTELLE

ITALY   SERVES: 6

*U*se the same batter as in "Singora Benzo's
Castagnaccio" recipe. Take small spoonfulls of the
batter and drop in a pan of hot oil. Fry until golden and
crispy on the outside. Drain and serve on a platter. Dust
with powdered sugar. These were served to my husband and
I by Signora Benzo, to whom I give my gratitude for her
hospitality.

POLENTA

*M*ost polentas today are made with corn meal. Though corn was introduced into Europe in the 16th century, "Poltos" was served long before in Greece and the Mediterranean. Corsica is known for its chestnut polenta. There are endless variations, ranging from sweet to savory. The ratio of chestnut flour to corn meal is not critical.

1/4 cup (50 g) finely chopped onion

1 Tablespoon olive oil

2/3 cup (100 g) corn meal

1/3 cup (60 g) chestnut flour

3 dried tomatoes

pinch of black pepper

1/4 teaspoon each of:
dried oregano
dried thyme
dried basil

3 cups (750 ml) chicken broth

2 Tablespoons *Parmesan* cheese grated

In a mixing bowl combine the first four ingredients. Slice the dried tomatoes into bits and add to the rest. Add the seasonings and mix well. Transfer to a sauce pan and stir in the chicken broth. Heat and let simmer until thickened, this may take 5-10 minutes. Stir to keep the bottom from sticking. Stir in the *Parmesan* cheese. Pour into a shallow pan or muffin tins no more than 1 inch (2.5 cm) thick and allow to cool in the refrigerator. Once cooled the congealed batter can be sliced and put on an olive oiled cookie sheet and baked at 325 F (165 C or gas 3) until browned. Serve while still warm.

SAVORY CHESTNUT CROQUETTES

COLONIAL AMERICA   SERVES: 4

1 lb. (450 g) fresh chestnuts

1 teaspoon minced onion

1/4 cup (60 ml) cream

2 Tablespoons (25 g) butter

3 eggs

1/2 cup (40 g) bread crumbs

oil for frying

Cut chestnuts in half and boil in enough water to cover for 15 minutes. Peel while still hot and mash with the onion, cream and butter with a potato masher until fairly smooth. Beat 2 of the eggs separately and then mix into the purée. Transfer the mixture to a double boiler and heat. Stir until thick, about 10 minutes. Set aside and let cool. When cool enough to handle, shape spoonfulls into cone shapes. Set these on a plate and refrigerate until firm. Beat the remaining egg. Dip the croquettes in the egg and then roll them in the breadcrumbs. Fry until golden brown and serve hot.

PERITAS DE CASTAÑA

SPAIN   SERVES: 4

*T*hese doughnuts are popular in many cultures and for good reason. Dust with powdered sugar and serve warm.

1 cup (140 g) pastry flour

1 cup (175 g) chestnut flour

1 teaspoon cinnamon

1 teaspoon baking powder

1/4 cup (55 g) sugar

3 eggs, separated

1/4 cup (60 ml) oil

1/2 cup (120 ml) milk

1/4 teaspoon vanilla extract

oil for frying

Sift the dry ingredients together. Separate the egg whites and yolks. Mix the yolks in a bowl with the oil, milk and vanilla. Beat the egg whites until stiff. Pour the yolk and milk mixture in with the dry ingredients and stir well to get out any lumps. Fold in the egg whites. Drop spoonfulls of the batter in hot oil deep enough for them to float. Fry until lightly golden and turn to fry both sides. Remove from hot oil with a slotted spoon and drain on paper. Sprinkle with powdered sugar. These are best served while still warm.

CHESTNUT PANCAKES

UNITED STATES   SERVES: 4

1 1/2 cups (210 g) sifted pastry flour

1/2 cups (80 g) sifted chestnut flour

1 teaspoon baking soda

2 eggs, separated

3 Tablespoons oil

1 3/4 cup (420 ml) milk

1/4 cup (60 ml) apple juice

Combine the flours and baking soda in a mixing bowl. Make a hole in the center of the flour and add 2 egg yolks and the oil. Beat the egg whites until stiff and set aside. Add the milk and then the juice and stir it all together to make the batter. Do not over mix for this will make a flat cake. Fold in the egg whites and immediatly drop large spoonfulls of the batter onto a hot, greased griddle. When the cakes begin to bubble, turn and cook the other side. Serve hot with maple syrup and apple butter.

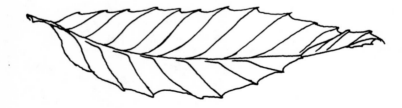

RAVIOLI CON RIPIENO DI CASTAGNE

ITALY   SERVES: 6

*T**his chestnut stuffed ravioli is a delicious Christmas dish served in Parma, where they take pride in their fruit mustards. I use homemade peach chutney, but any fruit chutney will do.*

4 cups (560 g) unbleached flour

4 large eggs

1 lb. (450 g) fresh chestnuts or 1/2 lb. (225 g) dried peeled chestnuts

2/3 cup (150 g) fruit chutney

3 Tablespoons pine nuts

1/2 lb. (225 g) *Parmesan* cheese freshly grated

Sift the flour into a mound on a smooth surface. Make a well in the mound and mix up the eggs in it. Slowly add flour from the mound to mix with the eggs. Continue to make a soft dough and knead until smooth. Cover with a lightly damp cloth and set aside. Roast and peel the chestnuts or prepare dried peeled chestnuts (see page 25 or 27). Mash or blend the chestnuts until fairly smooth. Lumps and small particles are okay. Blend this with the chutney and chopped pine nuts and set aside.

Roll the dough out into thin sheets and cut into 2 x 4 in. (5 x 10 cm) rectangles. Brush water on all edges of the rectangle. Place a small spoonfull of chestnut filling on one half of the dough and fold the other half over. Gently press out any air and seal the damp edges with the tines of a fork. Be certain not to pierce the dough. Cook in boiling water for about 5 minutes. Have a serving dish readied by sprinkling with grated *Parmesan*. Remove ravioli from boiling water with a slotted spoon and place on the cheese. Sprinkle more *Parmesan* on top. Serve hot.

CHESTNUT STUFFED MANICOTTI

ITALY   SERVES: 6

*R*olling your own fresh pasta dough is a satisfying task.
*I recommend using fresh sheets of pasta for this recipe.
Rolling the filling up in them is much easier than trying to
stuff the filling into the sides of store bought manicotti. Use
the ravioli pasta dough from the previous recipe.*

**1 1/4 lb. (560 g) fresh
    chestnuts or 2 cups (475 g)
    unsweetened purée.**
**18 manicotti shells or fresh
    sheets of pasta.**
2 shallots.
1 stalk celery.
2 Tablespoons olive oil.
1/4 cup (30 g) pine nuts
1 cup (250 ml) chicken broth
15 oz. (425 g) *Ricotta* cheese
1 egg
**3 Tablespoons fresh parsley
    chopped**
**1/2 teaspoon each of: thyme,
    taragon, marjoram.**
salt and pepper.
**3 Tablespoons (30 g)
    Mozzerella cheese grated.**

SAUCE:

3 Tablespoons olive oil
3 Tablespoons flour
3 cups (750 ml) chicken broth
**3 Tablespoons (40 ml) white
    wine**
4 oz. (120 ml) cream
salt and pepper

Preheat oven to 350 F (180
C or gas 4). Roast and peel
the fresh chestnuts (see
page 25) and form a purée
with a blender or sieve. If
using dry manicotti shells
boil for 3 minutes, drain and
rinse in cold water. Mince
the shallots and celery and
sauté in the olive oil until
soft. Add chopped pine
nuts, purée and chicken
broth and mix well. Remove
from heat and stir in the
Ricotta cheese, egg and
seasonings. Mix well and
keep warm.

Prepare the sauce by
heating the oil in a skillet
and brown the flour. Slowly
add chicken broth while
stirring. Once smooth, stir
in the wine, cream, salt and
pepper. Stir until thick and
smooth. Pour half of the
sauce in a large casserole
dish. Stuff the manicotti
shells with the filling and
lay side by side in the dish.
Laddle the remaining sauce
over the noodles, cover and
bake in a preheated oven for
45 minutes. During the last
10 minutes of baking,
uncover dish and sprinkle
with the *Mozzerella* cheese.
Serve hot.

Chapter Seven

DESSERTS

CHESTNUT TORTE

*T*his is a delicate dessert and a favorite of my friends who cannot tolerate wheat in their diet. The torte can be decorated with bits of candied chestnuts and an apricot glaze or thin ribbons of caramel.

1 1/2 lbs. (700 g) fresh chestnuts

1/2 cup (170 g) light honey

1/2 cup (110 g) butter melted

1 egg beaten

1 teaspoon vanilla extract

1/2 teaspoon ground cardamon

2 egg whites beaten stiff

Preheat oven to 325 F (170 C or gas 3). Purée chestnuts (see page 27). Add honey and butter and mix well. Add the whole beaten egg and flavorings. Mix well. Beat the egg whites until stiff peaks form and fold into the purée. Spoon the purée into an 8 inch (20 cm) greased spring form pan. Place in the preheated oven and bake for about 1 hour or until center is firm.

CHESTNUT ALMOND CAKE

TURKEY   SERVES: 6

1 lb. (450 g) fresh chestnuts

1/4 cup (50 g) butter melted

1 1/4 cups (300 ml) whole milk

1/4 teaspoon almond extract

1 cup (140 g) sifted pastry flour

1/2 teaspoon baking powder

handful of blanched almonds

Preheat oven to 350 F (180 C or gas 4). Purée chestnuts (see page 27). Stir in melted butter, milk and almond extract. Beat well. In a separate bowl sift the flour and baking powder together. Pour in the wet ingredients and mix vigorously. Pour into a greased 8 inch (20 cm) cake pan. Smooth with a spatula and decorate with the almonds by pressing them onto the surface. Bake in a preheated oven for about 1 hour or until firm. Serve with whip cream and coffee or hot cocoa.

Diable, used for roasting chestnuts. Europe

CHESTNUT PIE

SCOTLAND   SERVES: 6-8

*M*rs. McLintoc first published her "Receipts for Cookery and Pastry " in 1736 when, no doubt, her "Chestnut Pye" was quite popular. Though some "pye" it must have been, with two dozen apples, 100 chestnuts and several pounds of other nuts and fruits. Offered here is a version using more accessible ingredients and adapted for the modern kitchen. Dried chestnuts can be used, but the flavor of freshly roasted nuts really stands out.

2 cups (280 g) sifted pastry flour

10 oz. (275 g) sweet butter

5 Tablespoons (75 ml) ice water

3 large pie apples

20 chestnuts

1/4 cup (50 g) blanched sliced almonds

1/4 cup (50 g) raisins

3 Tablespoons orange zest

1/4 cup (60 grams) sugar

1/2 teaspoon nutmeg

2 teaspoons cinnamon

2 Tablespoons white wine

Grease a 9 inch (23 cm) pie pan and preheat the oven to 450 F (230 C or gas 8). For the crust, sift flour into a large bowl and cut in the butter using a fork or fingers until the dough is in pea sized bits. Slowly add the water and roll dough into a ball. Cut in half for a bottom and top. Roll out half for the bottom and place in the pan so the dough laps over the edges. For the filling, peel, core and thinly slice the apples, lightly roast and peel the chestnuts, and toss these with all the remaining ingredients in a bowl until well mixed. Transfer the filling into the crust, dot with additional bits of butter. Roll out the crust top and lay over it all. Pinch the edges and prick the top with a fork to vent the steam. Lightly sprinkle the pie with sugar (optional), and place in the oven. After the first 5 minutes reduce the heat to 350 F (180 C or gas 4) and bake for 40 minutes or until done.

MBULJUTA

MALTA   SERVES: 6

*O*ne *of the smallest nations of the world brings us this delightful pudding. Serve with a spoonfull of whipped cream and a thin slice of orange as a garnish.*

1 1/2 lbs. (700 g) fresh chestnuts

2 Tablespoons cocoa powder

1/3 cup (110 g) light honey

2 Tablespoons orange zest

2 Tablespoons Grand Marnier

Slice the chestnuts in half and boil (see page 26). Drain and peel while hot. Place chestnuts in a heavy saucepan and add enough fresh water to cover. Simmer on a low heat for about 15 minutes or until the chestnuts are very soft. Add the cocoa and honey and mash it all together. Continue simmering. Add the orange zest and Grand Marnier. Stir often and simmer until thick.

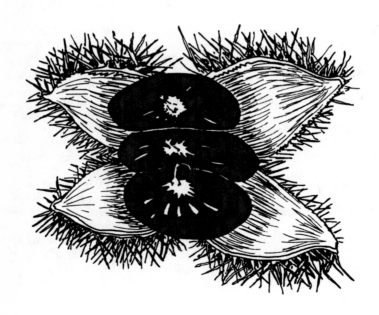

*T*he first ice creams ever created were by a French chef employed in the royal kitchens of Charles I of England in the 1650's. Though ices of all kinds had been popular for at least 100 years in Europe, this ice cream was so rich beyond compare that the King paid the chef to keep his recipe a secret from others. Since that time every possible combination of flavors has been explored in the making of ice creams. From the streetside cafés of Italy to the creameries of Philadelphia, chestnuts, whether they be candied, roasted or puréed, have found their way into this most favored treat.

ITALIAN CHESTNUT ICE CREAM

ITALY   SERVES: 6

3/4 cup (170 g) sugar

6 egg yolks

1 cup (250 ml) whole milk

2 cups (475 ml) heavy cream

1 Tablespoon vanilla extract

dash salt

3/4 cup (100 g) candied chestnut pieces

In a large bowl beat the sugar and egg yolks until smooth. Add the milk and beat well. Transfer to a double boiler on a medium heat. Stir frequently until thickened. This may take as long as 15 to 20 minutes. Do not allow the custard to boil. Remove from the heat and let cool by placing it in the refrigerator or by setting the top pan of the double boiler in a bowl of ice. Once cooled beat in the cream, vanilla extract and salt until very smooth. Transfer this to an ice cream machine and freeze according to manufacturer's directions. When the ice cream is nearly done add the candied chestnut pieces and then finish mixing.

EUROPEAN CHESTNUT ICE CREAM

EUROPE   SERVES: 6

*T*his recipe is identical to the Italian Chestnut Ice Cream recipe, except that one cup of unsweetened chestnut purée is added instead of, or as well as, the candied chestnut pieces. A very thick purée is required. The purée is added to the egg and milk mixture after it has cooked and as it is cooling.

ROASTED CHESTNUT ICE CREAM

UNITED STATES   SERVES: 6

*T*his ice cream has a completely unique taste due to the roasty flavor of the chestnuts.

1/2 lb. (225 g) fresh chestnuts

3/4 cup (170 g) sugar

6 egg yolks

1 cup (250 ml) whole milk

2 cups (475 ml) heavy cream

1 Tablespoons malted milk powder

1 Tablespoon vanilla extract

1/4 teaspoon salt

Roast and peel the chestnuts (see page 25) Chop into halves and quarters and set aside. In a large bowl beat the sugar and egg yolks until smooth. Add the milk and beat well. Transfer to a double boiler on a medium heat. Stir frequently until thickened. This may take as long as 15 to 20 minutes. Do not allow the custard to boil. Remove from the heat and let cool by placing in the refrigerator or by setting the top pan of the double boiler in a bowl of ice. Once cooled beat in heavy cream, malted milk powder, vanilla extract and salt. Transfer this to an ice cream machine and freeze according to manufacturer's directions. When the ice cream is nearly done, add the chestnut pieces and then finish mixing.

CHESTNUT ICE

ITALY

SERVES: 6

1 1/2 lbs. (700 g) fresh chestnuts

1 Tablespoon rum

2 1/4 cups (500 g) sugar

1/3 cup (70 ml) water

1 teaspoon vanilla extract

Boil and purée the chestnuts, (see page 27). Stir rum into the purée and place in the refrigerator. In a saucepan combine the sugar and water and heat to a temperature of 270 F (132 C), or when a small bit of syrup dropped into ice water forms hard threads. Remove from heat and mix the syrup into the purée. Add the vanilla extract. Let mixture cool and then process in an ice cream machine according to manufacturer's directions.

Toupin, used for blanching chestnuts. France

NESSLERODE PUDDING

EUROPE   SERVES: 8

*C*ount *Nesslerode, a prominant Russian diplomat of the
19th century must have loved chestnuts. His head chef,
Monsieur Moug, created an elaborate frozen chestnut custard
delight, forever after to be known as "Nesslerode Pudding".*

**2 oz. (50 g) candied or dried
cherries**

**2 oz. (50 g) candied or dried
pineapple**

3 oz. (75 g) *Sultana* raisins

3 oz. (80 ml) cognac or brandy

6 egg yolks

3/4 cup (170 g) sugar

2 cups (475 ml) whole milk

**1 cup (240 g) sweetened
chestnut purée**

1 teaspoon vanilla extract

1 cup (250 ml) heavy cream

Chop the cherries in half
and the pineapple into
small bits. Place all the
dried fruit in a glass or
ceramic bowl with the
cognac. Cover the bowl and
let sit over night. Beat the
egg yolks well and then beat
in the sugar until smooth.
Heat the milk to very hot,
but not boiling, and slowly
pour and stir into the egg
mixture. Once well beaten,
pour into a heavy bottomed
sauce pan and place on a low
heat. Stir continually until
thickened. Make certain the
custard does not boil.
Remove from the heat and
blend in the sweetened
chestnut purée and vanilla
extract. Drain the fruit and
mix into the custard. Beat
in the cream. Take 1 1/2
quart (1.5 liter) charlotte or
gellatin mold, (preferably a
plastic one with a tight
fitting lid) and lightly
grease the inside. Pour in
the custard. Place in the
freezer and let sit at least
overnight, until frozen.
Keep frozen until ready to
serve. Then remove from
freezer and dip in warm
water briefly to help release
it from the mold. Turn over
onto a chilled serving plate
and lift off the mold.
Decorate with whipped
cream, candied chestnuts
and/or candied fruits.

CHESTNUT CREAM

EASTERN EUROPE   SERVES: 4

*S*erved in Hungary, Austria, the former Yugoslavia,
*Russia and the Middle East, chestnut cream may be the
foundation of many fine inventive desserts. Simply served
in a fruit cup with a garnish of raspberries and whipped
cream or in tartlet shells with chocolate and Grand Marnier.
The cook is only limited by the imagination.*

**3/4 lb. (350 g) fresh chestnuts
or 1 cup (240 g) unsweetened
chestnut purée**

2 cups (450 g) sugar

1/2 cup (120 ml) water

1/2 cup (110 g) unsalted butter

1/2 cup (120 ml) heavy cream

1/2 teaspoon vanilla extract

If using fresh chestnuts,
process to make a purée (see
page 27). In a saucepan
combine the sugar and water
and bring to a boil. Cook
over a medium heat until
hardball stage is attained,
being at about 250 F (120 C).
When the syrup is ready,
remove from the heat and
emerse the bottom of the pot
in cold water to stop the
cooking, however, do not cool
the syrup. Add the syrup in
a fine stream slowly to the
purée, stirring all the while
until completely blended
and smooth. Mix in the
softened butter. Beat in the
cream and vanilla. Chill in a
pastry tube to fill tartlets,
or in a bowl to be scooped
into fruit cups once firm.

MONT BLANC

EUROPE   SERVES: 8

*T*his is a popular dessert in France, Italy and Switzerland. It is a festive treat which is shaped to honor the
mountain in the Alps known by the same name and shared
by the French, Italian and Swiss borders.

1 lb. (450 g) fresh chestnuts

2 cups (475 ml) milk

2 1 inch (3 cm) pieces vanilla bean

1 cup (225 g) granulated sugar

1/3 cup (110 g) light honey

1/4 cup (60 ml) water

1 Tablespoon unsalted butter

1 1/2 cups (350 ml) whipping cream

sweet chocolate shavings

Peel the chestnuts by boiling (see page 26). Place the peeled chestnuts in a saucepan. Add the milk and a section of the vanilla bean. Simmer on a low heat, covered for 30 minutes. Remove the vanilla bean and purée the chestnuts in a blender adding just enough of the milk to make a stiff purée. Meanwhile, in another pan cook sugar, water and the remaining section of the vanilla bean until softball stage of syrup, 235 F (112 C). Whip the hot syrup in with the purée. Beat in the butter. Let cool to firm. Form a mountain with the purée on a serving dish or in individual serving dishes. Whip the cream and smooth on the top of the mound. This is the snow cap of Mont Blanc. Sprinkle with the chocolate shavings and serve.

Mont Blanc maker. France

VERMICELLES AUX MARRONS

SWITZERLAND   SERVES: 8

se the same recipe as for "Mont Blanc" and add one tablespoon of Kirsch (cherry brandy) when mixing the purée. Press through a pastry tube onto individual serving dishes to form the "worms". Whipped cream is also served on top of this dessert.

PEKING DUST

CHINA   SERVES: 6

popular dessert in China and quite similar to the Mont Blanc.

2 lbs. (900 g) fresh chestnuts

1 cup (225 g) sugar

1 teaspoon vanilla extract

1 teaspoon sherry or Mirin

Chinese candied plums

candied lotus seeds

preserved kumquats

candied cherries

Make a purée with the chestnuts (see page 27). Stir in the sugar, vanilla and sherry. Mound the purée on a serving platter and form into the shape of a pyramid with a rubber spatula. Slice the candied fruits and decorate the purée. Chill and serve.

CHESTNUT DESSERT SOUFFLÉ

FRANCE   SERVES: 6

1 cup (140 g) candied chestnut pieces (see page 116)

2 Tablespoons Grand Marnier

1/4 cup (60 g) sugar

1/2 cup (70 g) sifted flour

dash salt

2 cups (475 ml) light cream

1 teaspoon vanilla extract

5 eggs separated

SAUCE:

3/4 cup (175 ml) whipping cream

1/2 cup (80 g) powdered sugar, sifted

3 Tablespoons Grand Marnier

1/4 teaspoon vanilla extract

Stir the Grand Marnier in with the candied chestnut pieces and set aside. In a saucepan, lightly stir the sugar, flour, and salt together. Mix in 1/2 cup (125 ml) of the cream. Once smooth add the rest of the cream and cook on a low heat until thickened. Remove from the heat and stir in the vanilla extract and the beaten yolks of the eggs. Stir in the chestnut pieces. Set aside to cool. Preheat oven to 350 F (180 C or gas 4). Butter a 9 inch (23 cm) soufflé dish and dust with powdered sugar. Whip the egg whites until stiff, but not dry. Fold them into the batter and then turn the batter into the soufflé pan. Bake for 25 minutes. Serve immediately with a Grand Marnier sauce. To make the sauce, whip the cream until stiff. Slowly add the sugar while beating, then add the Grand Marnier and then the vanilla. Pour over individual servings of the chestnut soufflé.

*E*uropeans have found many wonderful and diverse ways to create a chestnut compôte. Whether it be a medley of fruits and chestnuts to nourish the weak and elderly, or a rich dessert splashed with champagne to usher in the New Year, it is always a delight.

CHESTNUT COMPOTE

ITALY   SERVES: 4

*B*eing a very digestible and nutritious dish, this compote is reserved for convalescence of the weak and sickly.

1/2 lb. (225 g) fresh chestnuts, or 1/4 lb. (110 g) dried, peeled chestnuts

4 pitted prunes

4 halves dried pears

4 dried apricots

a small handfull raisins

1 stick cinnamon

1 1/2 cups (350 ml) water

Lightly roast and peel the chestnuts (see page 25). If using dried chestnuts, soak them overnight. Chop the dried fruit into strips. Combine all of the ingredients in a saucepan, cover and simmer on a low heat for 1 hour. Serve warm or cold.

CHESTNUTS IN CHAMPAGNE

AUSTRIA   SERVES: 4

Late autumn is often celebrated by indulging in roasted chestnuts and the early wines of the season, though the next morning may be a weary one. New Year's revelling also includes chestnuts, and with fond memories this recipe was related to me by one of my market customers.

1 lb. (450 g) fresh chestnuts

1 Tablespoon butter

dash of salt

1 cup (175 g) pitted prunes

1/2 cup (120 ml) water

1 cup (250 ml) champagne

whipped cream

Roast and peel the chestnuts (see page 25). In a saucepan lightly sauté the chestnuts in the butter and salt. Add the prunes and water and simmer with the lid on for 20 minutes. Stir in the champagne and heat until quite warm. Serve warm in dessert cups with whipped cream topping.

GREEK CHESTNUT COMPOTE

GREECE   SERVES: 6

1 lb. (450 g) fresh chestnuts

1 cup (225 g) sugar

zest from 1 lemon (grated outer layer of peel)

1 cup (250 ml) water

1/2 teaspoon vanilla extract

Lightly roast and peel the chestnuts (see page 25). Simmer the nuts in enough water to cover until tender, but not mushy, about 8 minutes. In another pot heat the sugar, lemon zest, and water. Let thicken to a syrup and add the drained chestnuts. Coat the nuts with the syrup and simmer gently for 10 minutes. Add the vanilla and serve warm.

APPLE AND CHESTNUT COMPOTE

GERMANY   SERVES: 4-6

1/2 lb. (225 g) fresh chestnuts

3 *Granny Smith* apples

1 lemon

1/2 cup (120 ml) water

3 Tablespoons honey

2 Tablespoons white wine

whipped cream

Roast and peel the chestnuts (see page 25). Peel, core and slice the apples into slender wedges. Zest and juice the lemon. Combine all ingredients except the wine in a sauce pan and simmer with a lid over a low heat for 10 minutes. Add the wine and chill. Serve with whipped cream.

CANDIED CHESTNUTS

FRANCE   MAKES 2 DOZEN

Candied chestnuts can be used in many ways. The whole nuts can be dipped in chocolate or caramel. The chestnut pieces can be used in confections and soufflés. They also make a nice decoration on tortes, tarts and cakes.

1 lb. (450 g) fresh chestnuts

12 cups (3 liters) water

2 cups (450 g) sugar

1 teaspoon vanilla extract

1 Tablespoon rum, cognac or Grand Marnier

Lightly roast and peel the chestnuts (see page 25), trying not to break them. In a large pot heat the water and sugar. Once the water begins to boil add the chestnuts and then turn down the heat to a gentle simmer. Cover and continue cooking for about 3 hours. Remove the lid and continue to simmer until the syrup is thick. Stir occasionally to keep the nuts coated. Add the vanilla extract and liquor. Cool and store in a jar in the refrigerator. May be stored for 2 weeks.

ALGERIAN CHESTNUT JAM

ALGERIA   MAKES 7 - 1/2 PINT JARS

Chestnuts grow on the slopes of the Atlas mountain range of Northern Africa. This recipe includes orange blossom water, which attests to the Arabic influence of that region.

2 lbs. (900 g) fresh chestnuts

4 cups (1 kg) sugar

6 Tablespoons (80 ml) orange blossom water

Gently roast and peel chestnuts (see page 25), taking care not to break them up too much. Place the nuts in a saucepan, add enough water to cover them and simmer on a low heat for about 20 to 30 minutes. The nuts need to be well cooked but not mushy. Drain well. Combine the sugar and orange blossom water in a sauce pan. Heat and stir until the sugar dissolves. Add the chestnuts and cook until syrup is thick. Pour into hot sterile jars and seal with sterile lids. Store in the refrigerator for up to 6 weeks.

CHESTNUT AND FIG CONSERVES

ITALY   MAKES 7 - 1/2 PINT JARS

1/2 lb. (225 g) fresh chestnuts

3/4 lb. (350 g) dried figs

2 lbs. (900 g) pears

3 Tablespoons orange zest
(grated outer layer of peel)

6 oz. (175 ml) fresh squeezed
orange juice

1 1/2 cups (350 g) sugar or 3/4
cups (255 g) honey

1 cinnamon stick

12 cloves

3 allspice

2 pieces candied ginger

1/4 cup (60 ml) Grand Marnier

Roast and peel the chestnuts (see page 25). Stem the figs and peel and core the pears. Chop all of the above coarsely and place in a large heavy pot. Add the zest, juice, sugar or honey and begin to simmer over a low heat, covered. Place the cinnamon, cloves and allspice in a piece of clean cheesecloth and tie shut. Drop this into the pot. Stir often and simmer for at least 30 minutes. Chop the candied ginger fine and add to the conserve. Stir in the Grand Marnier and simmer for 5 more minutes. Ladle into sterile jars and once cooled, store in the refrigerator or freezer. Due to the low levels of sugar and acid in this conserve, it must be processed in a pressure canner to store on the shelf. After packing in sterile jars and screwing down sterile lids tight, process for 15 minutes at 10 pounds pressure (at sea level).

MARRON GLACÉ

ITALY   MAKES 20 CANDIES

*B*iting into these sweet creamy bits of chestnut heaven *will cause an involuntary moan of delight every time. It's no wonder they are historically so prized by the elite and noble class. The French will tell you that they were the first to create the Marron Glacé and the best in the world are made from French marrones by French chefs. Now, if you were to ask an Italian about Marron Glacé, you would learn that it is one of the greatest of Italian delicasies dating far back into antiquity and only the best are made from the Italian marroni. The creation of these precious candies is a prideful art and can take years to master. Not only does the process take much time and patience, a specific type of chestnut must be used, that being the marron. Chestnut kernals must meet strict requirements to qualify as a 'marron'. These include size, shape, texture and peelability. One of the secrets to successful Marron Glacé, is in using marron quality chestnuts.*

1 lb. (450 g) firm *Marroni*
   chestnuts
1/4 teaspoon citric acid
2 1/2 cups (560 g) sugar
2 1/2 cups (600 ml) water
vanilla bean

Scrub the chestnuts with a vegetable brush, rinse and place unshelled, in a glass bowl. Fill with enough cold water to cover the nuts and stir in the citric acid. Place in refridgerator for 1 week. Drain off water and peel the outer shell. Gently place the nuts in boiling water just long enough to loosen the pellicle (inner, papery, brown skin), about 5 minutes. In a large non-metalic saucepan, mix the sugar and water for the syrup and place on a low heat. Add the vanilla bean and once the syrup begins to simmer, gently add the chestnuts. Maintain a very gentle simmer. Cover with a lid and process this way for 48 hours, basting the nuts from time to time. Remove the nuts from the syrup with a slotted spoon and place on a sieve to drain and cool. Preheat oven at 550 F (290 C or gas 9). Place the nuts on a flame proof rack and bake for 1 1/2 minutes. This removes the stickiness and seals the nuts. Let them cool and individually wrap in waxed paper and foil. These may be stored in a cool dry place for up to one month. The nuts are also very nice dipped in chocolate before they are wrapped.

CHESTNUT CRESCENTS

UNITED STATES   MAKES 2 DOZEN

6 Tablespoons (75 g) unsalted butter

1/4 cup (60 g) sugar

1 egg yolk

1/2 cup (240 g) unsweetened chestnut purée

1/2 teaspoon vanilla extract

1 cup (140 g) pastry flour

1/4 teaspoon cinnamon

1 small pinch of salt

1/2 cup (100 g) semi-sweet chocolate chips

Preheat oven to 350 F (180 C or gas 4). Blend the softened butter and the sugar well. Beat in the egg yolk. Mix in the chestnut purée and the vanilla extract. Sift the flour, cinnamon and salt and then stir into the creamed mixture. The dough should be just firm enough to handle with floured fingers. Pinch off a small piece at a time and roll into a crescent shape. Place on a lightly greased cookie sheet and bake for 15 minutes or until lightly browned. Place on a rack to cool. Put the cookies in the freezer to freeze. Melt the chocolate chips in a double boiler and dip one half of each frozen cookie in the chocolate. Lay on plastic wrap until cooled. Store in a cool dry place.

CROATIAN CHESTNUT CAKE

CROATIA   SERVES: 8

3 lbs. (1.35 kg) fresh chestnuts

2/3 cup (150 g) sugar

1 1/3 cup (300 g) softened
unsalted butter

1 cup (200 g) semi-sweet
chocolate chips

cocoa powder

whipped cream

Purée the chestnuts (see page 27), adding as little water as possible to create a very stiff purée. Beat in the sugar and 2/3 cup (150 grams) softened butter. Cover with plastic wrap and place in the refrigerator overnight. In a double boiler, melt the chocolate chips and the remaining butter, mixing well. Remove from heat and let cool. Take the chestnut purée and roll out into a rectangle about 1/2 to 3/4 inch (1.5 to 2 cm) thick onto plastic wrap which has been lightly dusted with cocoa powder. Spread 3/4 of the melted chocolate over this and carefully roll up. Take the last of the chocolate and warm it up enough to spread like an icing over the top of the roll. Instead of a roll, this same cake can be made into a square shape with many layers begining with the chestnut at the bottom and finishing with the chocolate on the top. Serve with whipped cream. If well wrapped, this cake may be stored in the refrigerator for up to 5 days, or can also be frozen.

BÛCHE DE NOEL

FRANCE   SERVES: 8

*The longest nights of the year were illuminated by the
yule log, burning bright from time immemorial. This
yule log is made with chestnuts, chocolate and rum and
traditionally is decorated to resemble a log, complete with
bark, leaves, berries, nuts and even mushrooms. To decorate
this holiday specialty, use nuts, candied or dried fruits,
colored marzipan berries, chocolate leaves and powdered
sugar for snow. The mushrooms are made from sweet meringue. The caps and stems are formed separately by
forcing the meringue through a pastry tube onto baking
paper and dried in a cool oven for about 2 hours. The cap is
then placed on top of the stem and dusted with cocoa powder. The plate is often garnished with fern, cedar, or holly
leaves (being certain to remove any real holly berries).*

2 lbs. (900 g) fresh chestnuts

1 cup (100 g) sweet chocolate chips

1/4 cup (60 g) sugar

1/2 cup (110 g) unsalted butter

1 Tablespoon rum

cooking oil

Purée the chestnuts(see page 27), adding very little water to create a stiff paste. Melt the chocolate over a double boiler. While still warm, blend the chocolate into the chestnut purée. Blend in the sugar and when mixed, add the softened butter. Blend well and stir in the rum. Refridgerate until cooled. Spread out a sheet of waxed paper or plastic wrap and rub with the oil to cover lightly. Place the dough in the center of the paper. Bring the paper up around 2 opposite sides and roll back and forth to form a log shape. The log should be about a foot (30 cm) long. Wrap up well and refrigerate overnight. When ready to present, unwrap carefully and lay on the serving dish. Run a fork lengthwise along the log to create bark. Cut off the ends at an angle and decorate. Slices may be served in a puddle of raspberry sauce and whipped cream.

MARRONS FLAMBÉ

FRANCE   SERVES: 6

A̶lso known as "Chestnuts au feu de Lucifer", this flaming dessert adds a dramatic finish to an elegant dinner.

1 lb. (450 g) fresh chestnuts

3 cups (700 ml) water

3/4 cup (250 g) light honey

1 piece vanilla bean

1/2 cup (120 ml) good rum or brandy

1 lb. (450 g) fruit cake

1 qt. (1 liter) vanilla ice cream

Lightly roast and peel the chestnuts (see page 25). In a saucepan boil the water, honey and vanilla bean for 15 minutes, covered. Add the chestnuts and half of the rum. Simmer gently for 15 or 20 minutes, trying not to break the nuts. Remove from the heat and let set for an hour or two, (or while you are peparing and eating dinner). Return to the heat and warm through, about 5 minutes. Remove the vanilla bean. Meanwhile, arrange slices of fruit cake on a serving dish. Heap the candied chestnuts over the fruit cake and spoon the syrup over it all. Warm the remaining rum and pour over the chestnuts and cake. Have matches ready and light the chestnuts immediately. Serve with the ice cream.

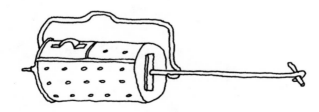

Chestnut roaster, Europe

CHESTNUT RESOURCES

The American Chestnut Foundation

A non-profit organization. Their goal is to restore the American chestnut to its native forests through breeding and research.

The American Chestnut Foundation
469 Main Street, P.O. Box 4044
Bennington, VT 05201-4044, U.S.A.
Phone: (802) 447-0110
E-mail: chestnut@acf.org
Online at: *http://www.acf.org*

The American Chestnut Cooperators' Foundation

A nonprofit scientific and educational foundation dedicated to restoring the American chestnut to its former place in our Eastern hardwood forests.

ACCF
2667 Forest Service Road 708
Newport, VA 24128, U.S.A.
Online at: *http://ipm.ppws.vt.edu/griffin/accf.html*

The Canadian Chestnut Council

A charitable organization that has been actively involved since 1988 in the development and implementation of numerous objectives in support of the American chestnut.

Dr. Colin D. McKeen, Chairman
62 Westmorland Ave.
Orangeville, ON, L9W 3B6, CANADA
Online at: *http://www.uoguelph.ca/~chestnut/index.htm*

Chestnut Growers of Australia Ltd.

Dedicated to the growth of the chestnut industry through grower education, promotion, research, and sharing of information.

Industry Development Officer: Susan Benedyka

Chestnut Growers of Australia Ltd.

P.O. Box 4

Chiltern Vic 3683, AUSTRALIA

Phone: (03) 5726 1155; Fax: (03) 5726 1174

Email: s.benedyka@bigpond.com

Online at: *http://www.chestnutgrowers.com.au*

Midwest Nut Producers Council

A non-profit organization founded in 1992 to enhance the region's commercial nut industry through education, research and promotion of nuts and the tree species and varieties that bear nuts.

Dennis W. Fulbright

Department of Plant Pathology

Michigan State University

East Lansing, MI 48824-1312, U.S.A.

Email: fulbrig1@msu.edu

online at: *http://www.chestnutgrower.org*

Northern Nut Growers Association

A national non-profit organization with members throughout the U.S. and 15 foreign countries. It was founded in 1911 to share information on nut tree growing. Members include beginning nut culturists, farmers, amateur and commercial nut growers, experiment station workers, horticultural teachers and scientists, nut tree breeders, nurserypeople, and foresters.

Online at: *www.northernnutgrowers.org* or *www.nutgrowing.org*

The New Zealand Chestnut Council, Inc.

The nationally recognized product group for chestnuts of New Zealand. The aim of NZCC is to encourage, promote and advance New Zealand's Chestnut Industry.

David Klinac (Executive Director)
NZCC
P.O. BOX 19250
Hamilton, NEW ZEALAND
Phone: 07-856 9321
Email: dklinac@hortresearch.co.nz; rbb@clear.net.nz
Online at: *http://www.nzcc.org.nz*

Western Chestnut Growers Assn., Inc.

WCGA was incorporated in 1996 to promote chestnuts in Western North America. Their mission is to disseminate information to growers, provide a means of communication within the industry, support research and breeding work, and generally to further the interests and knowledge of growers. They welcome new members from any part of the world.

WCGA
P.O. Box 841
Ridgefield, WA 98642, U.S.A.
Online at: *http://www.wcga.net*

Printed in the United States
78265LV00002B/31

9 781587 361678